STRING of PEARLS

STRING *of* PEARLS

(((ON THE NEWS BEAT IN
NEW YORK AND PARIS)))

Priscilla L. Buckley

WITH AN AFTERWORD BY
William F. Buckley Jr.

ILLUSTRATIONS BY
Lee Buckley

THOMAS DUNNE BOOKS
ST. MARTIN'S PRESS
NEW YORK

THOMAS DUNNE BOOKS.
An imprint of St. Martin's Press.

STRING OF PEARLS. Copyright © 2001 by Priscilla L. Buckley. All rights reserved.
Printed in the United States of America. No part of this book may be used or repro-
duced in any manner whatsoever without written permission except in the case of
brief quotations embodied in critical articles or reviews. For information, address St.
Martin's Press, 175 Fifth Avenue, New York, N.Y. 10010.

www.stmartins.com

BOOK DESIGN BY CASEY HAMPTON

ISBN 0-312-27217-0

First Edition: April 2001

10 9 8 7 6 5 4 3 2 1

To my best friends, my siblings:
Jim, Jane, Bill, Trish, Reid, Carol,
and my siblings-in-law:
Ben, Pat, Ann, Tasa, Gerry, and Seton,
but particularly to
Jane

STRING *of* PEARLS

(((PART ONE)))

NEW YORK

1944-1948

I OPENED THE DOOR and walked into a scene of controlled chaos. The United Press newsroom on the twelfth floor of the Daily News Building in New York was at the time the largest newsroom in the world: several hundred men at hundreds of battered typewriters arranged in great Us—a U for each department—and dozens of teletype machines ringing and clattering day and night, erupting with news from all over the world. The editor sat at the outside of the U, the assistant editor faced him across the desk in what was called "the slot," and the rewritemen and reporters manned typewriters along the long arms of the U. The floors were littered with paper, cigarette butts, and the desks with graying, cooling, stained containers of coffee, empty Coke bottles, paper, pipes, debris. A haze of smoke hung over the scene; cigarettes dangled from lips or perched perilously on the edge of tables. Paper spewed from the open mouths of huge wastebaskets. The floor was filthy, debris smashed flat underfoot.

The shirtsleeved men kept their eyes on their machines as I

walked down the long line of typewriters past the foreign desk where a tall skinny fellow with glasses looked up and almost nodded before turning back to the copy at hand. He was Harrison Salisbury, who would soon take over the job as foreign editor. Walter Cronkite had recently departed the scene to serve as a UP war correspondent in Europe. It was early January 1944.

Near the end of the room, an alcove on the left housed UP's Radio News Department. Here was another U-shaped cluster of long and short tables, half a dozen men at their typewriters too busy to look up, and in the corner of the room, by the window, a couple of proper desks. Leaning way back in a chair at one of them, his feet comfortably resting on the desktop, arms behind his head, a picture of relaxation in a scene of restrained turmoil: Phil Newsom, chief of the radio desk, the man with whom I had an appointment. Newsom was in his late thirties, good-looking, with a reddish complexion (martinis) and blue eyes that were enhanced by his startling white hair.

I introduced myself. "Priscilla Buckley," I said. "Are you Mr. Newsom?"

He sat up and invited me to sit down and very kindly, very gently, interviewed me. Yes, I was a recent Smith College graduate. (He took my word for it. I had filled out no forms.) Yes, I had worked on the college newspaper. (Even I knew enough not to press that point.) I had heard about the job opening for a copy girl through a college friend who was herself a copy girl at Associated Press in Rockefeller Center. No, I had never held a job before. Mr. Newsom explained to me that working for a news organization was not like any other job, and that I should understand that it had many drawbacks. It had no regular hours. You could be asked to work any shift around the clock. And there were no proper weekends. They tried to give everyone two consecutive days off every week, but it would be a long time, and maybe never, before I could expect a Saturday and Sunday off. The pay, he commented, was not good, although he didn't mention a figure. Finally he told me that the job I was asking for had been filled a day earlier, but he would take my name and address in case that didn't work out. We shook hands and I retired back through that long, busy newsroom and out the door where the receptionist, the only woman I had seen in my brief foray, asked how the interview had gone, and I confessed that I had not gotten the job. She said she was sorry.

We Were the Lucky Ones

It was years before I realized how lucky I was to be looking for a job just then, in January of 1944. Two years earlier, a third of the way through my junior year at Smith College, Japan had struck Pearl Harbor, and suddenly we were at war. Within weeks the campus scene had changed. Hundreds, thousands of young men dropped out of college and enlisted, and within months those who hadn't were being signed up in all sorts of service programs as all branches of the military, with a world war on their hands, rushed to enlist college-level recruits for the officer corps needed to move from peacetime to wartime strength.

At Smith, my senior year, over a hundred of my classmates had enlisted in the brand-new WAVES, the women's corps of the U.S. Navy, and girls I used to share a Coke or a malted milk with at the Corner Drug now marched in their neat blue uniforms, lisle stockings, and sensible shoes from dorm to mess hall to class to drill field in formation, looking neither left nor right. There was a feeling of urgency on the campuses to get on with life's work. Betty Goldstein (later Friedan), who had edited the Smith College newspaper the year I joined it, and who was a year ahead of me, was already in New York working for International Press. The rest of us wanted in, too. What none of us realized was that because at the height of the hostilities nearly eleven million young American men were in uniform, jobs in the civil economy that would have been closed to women two years earlier, and would be closed to them three years later when the veterans came home, were there for the plucking. Employers were desperate for help and we were the only help in sight, young women, girls really, in the graduating college classes of '42, '43, '44, and '45. We were the lucky ones.

Book of Knowledge

That afternoon I applied for another job that one of my helpful Smith friends had told me about. It was at *The Book of Knowledge*. My brothers and sisters, as many others in our generation, had grown up with *The Book of Knowledge*, a wonderful encyclopedia for children that was great to look things up in, but greater still to browse about in. The editors of the encyclopedia were in the process of bringing *The Book of Knowledge* up-to-date for a new edition and the job that I had heard about would be to rewrite the fairy tales and other stories in more modern and somewhat more understandable language. An extremely nice Mrs. Foster, I believe that was her name, interviewed me. This time I did fill out a simple form (family, educational background, date of birth, religion, and so on). She asked me to write a thousand-word piece on some thing or event that would be of interest to a young audience and to bring it in as soon as possible, the next day if I could manage it, since they were anxious to fill the job.

I rushed home to the Phoebe Warren House, a woman's boardinghouse where I was living with my sister Patricia, who was finishing off her senior year at the Nightingale-Bamford School in New York. I took out the portable Royal typewriter father had given me freshman year at Smith, insuring that I would learn to touch-type by having its letter keys blacked out. The numbered keys had not been blacked out, and to this day I have to look down when I type a number or depress the shift key and reach for @ # % ^ & * ( ) – +.,

A month or so earlier some of my siblings and I had made the arduous journey from Mexico City to Morelia and thence by jeep and mule and foot to the site of the volcano of Paricutín, which had erupted several months earlier and was now a mountain several hundred feet high. It had been a fascinating excursion—and touching, too, when you rode past a row of small wooden crosses the *campesinos* had raised to divert the flow of lava from their adobe villages. I thought this might be a new and different kind of a story, and started to type.

On Thursday I got a call from Mrs. Foster. She liked my piece and was offering me the job, starting the following Monday, at $35 a week. Friday morning, a telegram from Mr. Newsom. The copy girl had quit. Could I start Monday morning? The pay was $18.50 a week! In 1944, $18.50 bought more than it does today, but not *that* much more.

What to do? There had been something terribly exciting about the glimpse of the UP newsroom. So, with gay abandon, I tossed aside *The Book of Knowledge*'s security and a living salary, and opted for UP, starvation wages, and a wonderful life. Rich I did not become from the labor of my brow, but neither have I ever been bored.

New York, New York, It's a Wonderful Town

In those days New York was the Mecca for the young and ambitious: it was where the action was. The very street names acted as magnetic poles. Want a career in business, in law, in finance? Head for Wall Street. In advertising? Madison Avenue. Publishing? Here were *Time*, *Life*, *Fortune*, *The New Yorker*, and a slew of the major book houses. (Boston still had a few.) Show biz? Broadway and Forty-second Street. Music? The Met, Carnegie Hall, Juilliard, and for the lower-browed, Fats Waller up in Harlem, Nick's in the Village, and Jimmy Ryan on West Fifty-second Street. Art? The Metropolitan Museum, the Frick, and the Whitney, and the new and exciting Museum of Modern Art. Journalism? New York sported a dozen scrappy newspapers, among them the *Sun*, the *News*, the *Mirror*, the *Journal-American*, *World-Telegram*, and *Trib*, plus the staid *New York Times*. "New York, New York," we all sang, "it's a wonderful town."

New York was big, exciting, bustling, clean, and safe. There was little street crime, certainly in Manhattan where we youngsters congregated.

It was a tidy kind of a city. The Italians lived in Little Italy and the Chinese in Chinatown. Writers, artists, poets, students, and kids settled in and around Greenwich Village where apartments were cheap and landlords permissive. The Germans were in Yorkville, in and around East Eighty-sixth Street. The blacks, who were called Negroes then, were mostly in Harlem and the Bronx. The homeless, who were called bums, hung out in the Bowery near the flophouses, soup kitchens, and municipal bath-

New York was the Mecca for the young and ambitious.

houses. Jews ran all of the delis that the Germans didn't, as well as the newspaper stands and stores. Italians were greengrocers, tailors, and cobblers. The Chinese did the laundry. The French ran cramped little restaurants—Le Bistro, Chez Jacques, La Grillade, Le Coin Normand—where you could get tasty three-course meals for a couple of dollars. We weren't interested in who ran Wall Street and the banks because we knew little about the first and dealt sparingly with the second. The Irish owned, staffed, and patronized the corner bar, and patrolled the streets.

There was little or no crime, aside from the front pages of the *News* or *Mirror*. It was known that jazz musicians—especially the drummers—got high on heroin and cocaine, but drugs played no part in most people's lives. There was poverty—there is always poverty—but it was not much in evidence.

New York was also a nickel-and-dime city, where youngsters

making twenty, thirty, and forty bucks a week could have a whale of a good time. Subways were swift, clean, graffiti-free, and safe, and they cost a nickel, as did most buses and the clattering, clanking elevated trains that ran north and south up and down Third Avenue. (Rents along Third, given that all conversation had to be suspended every minute or two as a train roared by, were cheap. That's where lots of us lived.) The Fifth Avenue buses were so grand they cost a dime, but in spring, summer, and fall you could ride on the open top deck of a double-decker bus all the way up Fifth Avenue and Riverside Drive feasting your eyes on the river traffic along the Hudson and marveling in the twilight as the lights outlined the airy gracefulness of the George Washington Bridge. Fifty cents at the Automat, ten buffalo nickels, could buy you a chicken pot pie (five nickels), a lemon meringue pie (three nickels), a glass of milk, and a cup of coffee (a nickel each).

We lived on what would now be called the poverty level, but didn't know it. (We did know enough, however, not to permit our parents to visit our apartments lest they give us The Look.) New York was our town. It was the tops! and so (we thought in our secret hearts) were we by the very fact that it had taken us in. To make it in New York, even at the bottom of the ladder, was to be in the Big Time. Every Broadway show told us that.

Collitchgirls

I arrived promptly Monday morning, shortly before nine A.M., inappropriately attired in a tailored suit, frilly white blouse, with hat and gloves and a navy blue purse that matched my high-heel shoes. Mr. Newsom was not yet in; he wouldn't arrive for another couple of hours. As I stood around uncertainly one of the shirtsleeved men at a typewriter noticed me. (Dick Amper was the noticing type) "You the new copy girl?" he asked. I nodded. "Bobby," he called, raising his voice. "Oh, Bobby, come here for a minute." From the back of the room a tall girl in sloppy smeared white blouse, shirttail half out, loped over. "What's your name?" Mr. Amper asked me. "Priscilla Buckley," I said, "but most people call me Pitts." "This is Bobby Ober," he said. "She'll tell you what to do," and he turned back to his typewriter.

Bobby was about eighteen, with a huge mouth and a broad smile that revealed uneven teeth. She shook hands and happily undertook my education, which meant that when anyone called for anything she sent me to do it, and went back to what must have been a most engrossing story in the *Daily News,* which had just been delivered by another copy boy. A copy girl was the equivalent of an office boy: you ran errands for the editors, went out to pick up drinks (soft) and sandwiches for the newsmen, changed the big rolls of teletype paper when they were in danger of running out, suffering verbal abuse if a word was lost in the transition from old to new roll. We sharpened pencils, ran out to the newstands to pick up the latest edition of every paper then printed in the city, and even, occasionally, emptied ashtrays that had disappeared beneath volcanic ash. (We were never instructed to do this; it was just that we couldn't stand the sight and smell of it.) It wasn't much fun.

Most of the handful of remaining copy boys at United Press were overaged underachievers, content to stay put in a no-future situation because they didn't aspire any higher. The copy girls, who were new to the enterprise, were something else again. For one thing they had aspirations: they wanted to be newspapermen. By most of the older newshands, we were, at least in those early days, contemptuously dismissed as *collitch-girls*, the syllables strung together in obloquy. *"Collitchgirl,"* sighed LeRoy Pope, who was riding the slot that first day when I went over to take his lunch order: "Another *collitchgirl!"*

Weeks later when the World War II manpower pinch had become so bad that I had been moved to the sports desk (over the all-but-dead body of the sports editor), LeRoy, again in the slot on a hot Sunday afternoon, would have his deepest suspicions of the inadequacy of *collitchgirls* confirmed. After he had responded to a dozen angry bells—complaints from local bureaus that something was wrong in a baseball score—and corrected my error, he stood up in the slot, brought his ruler down with a resounding slap that brought every head sharply around, and put me straight on how things work in the news world. "Pitts Buckley," he roared, "you can call Franklin Delano Roosevelt a goddamn sonovabitch, but you can't make a mistake in a baseball score!" He was absolutely right.

The Sports Desk

It was made clear to me when I was promoted to the sports desk ($25 a week) that I was never to mention my current assignment to anyone. What would editors around the country think if they knew that UP was so hard up it had had to assign a woman to the sports beat? My copy—even the nightly feature stories—went unsigned, or signed by the sports editor, and if a radio station or a UP bureau called for clarification of any point, I was instructed to call a copy boy and have him take the telephone while I dug up the needed information. He would then transmit it.

I didn't like my boss, the sports editor. His name was Bud Watson and he was a rarity in the news world: he was pompous and fussy and full of himself. Shifts came and went on the radio desk, and when you arrived you sat at whatever desk was empty and used that typewriter, those pencils, any eraser or handy stapler within reach, and if you went to the john and returned to find someone else at your desk, you simply moved over to another of the rickety Royal, Remington, and Underwood uprights that looked as if they had been bought about the time of the Civil War.

But not Bud Watson. Bud insisted that a man (of his rank and importance) needed his own desk, a typewriter reserved for his exclusive use, and a drawer in which he could lock his possessions when he departed the office in the evening. This the rest of us found preposterous, making Bud the target of innumerable practical jokes. A common trait of newspapermen is that they engage in childish practical jokes from which they derive immense amusement. One overnight shift—outraged by a snotty note Bud had written informing them that he had locked the roller of his typewriter in his desk drawer since he couldn't count on their complying with his civil request that they NOT USE HIS TYPEWRITER—spent hours planning a suitable revenge. When not otherwise engaged that night, they operated on his cherished Royal with a tiny screwdriver, loosening the screws that attached each letter— q w e r t y u i o p—to its support. Then they cunningly rearranged

They operated on his cherished Royal.

them, putting the *y* where the *t* should have been, the *u* where the *y* should have been, and so on. The day staff, which had been alerted to the caper, tingled with happy anticipation when Bud walked in that morning and, having first wiped off the top of his desk with his handkerchief, unlocked his drawer and replaced his roller, sat down, and pulled his chair up to the typewriter. After consulting his muse for a moment, he wrote: "With the opening day of the 1944 football season . . ." and only then glanced up to read what appeared on the page, to wit: "Eoyj yjr p]rmomh fsu pg yjr 1944 gppyns:: drsmpm . . ." Someone ripped the sheet out of the typewriter and passed it around. The newsroom exploded in laughter and even George Marder, on the desk, usually the soberest of characters, joined in the general hilarity. One lowlife was heard to remark that he had no idea Watson could be so eloquent.

Fun 'n' Games

A classic newspaper joke, to which I was not subjected, but to which a few of my friends were, was the chase for the "paper stretcher." An editor would call a copy boy and say that he needed his paper stretcher right away, but that it was on loan to Joe Smaltz at the *Trib*. "Run over and tell Joe I need it back."

Kill that story! Kill that story!

Out the door would go the copy boy or girl, to the *Trib* where Joe would say, "Gee, I am sorry, but Ed Metz at the *Brooklyn Eagle* needed one in a hurry last week and I sent it over." On to the *Brooklyn Eagle*, and the *Sun*, and the *World-Telegram*, and the next paper until a bright light flashed and the copy boy finally got the message. There was no such thing as a "paper stretcher." What the slower ones then did was to return sheepishly to the office and the not unkind laughter of the staff. What the smarter ones did was to take in a movie and report back just before the end of that particular shift, having left the pranksters in the lurch.

Two staffers on the city desk had a great thing going with the yokels who would crowd the ground floor of the *Daily News* building to watch the renowned, huge revolving globe in its well in the middle of the floor. These particular bozos would fortify themselves with a couple or so drinks at Sellman's bar and eatery across Forty-second Street, and when well tanked, go into their act. The first, his fedora on his head, and a large PRESS sign tucked in the hatband, and carrying a bunch of manila paper in his hand, would race through the ground story of the building, past the globe and the excited tourists, yelling: "Scoop! Scoop!" and head for the elevators. Minutes later, Bozo number two, also attired with a fedora and a PRESS sign, would race in yelling: "Kill that story! Kill that story!" and head for the elevator. Thirty minutes later, they might well repeat the scene to an entirely different audience.

Sunday is a slow news day unless there is a major catastrophe—fires, floods, shipwrecks, earthquakes, erupting volcanoes, that kind of thing—and the office in consequence was usually at half staff and the pace low-key. This particular Sunday, as we lazily perused the morning papers, someone got a laugh over a blooper in the *Herald Tribune*. On a feature page there were two stories, one about Congressman Hamilton Fish, a leader of the America First movement prior to Pearl Harbor, and a second about the arrival of a new consignment of tropical fish in the New York Aquarium. The captions had been reversed.

It was either Ed Korry or Arnold Dibble, I don't remember which, who decided to rib the *Trib* editors about the boner. He called, identified himself as Mr. Fish, and asked to speak to the managing editor because he felt an apology was owed him. The editor came on the line and said that he was somewhat con-

This is Mr. Tropical Fish

fused by the call since he had talked to Mr. Fish at some length earlier in the day and had promised to correct the error. Then, he asked, rather sharply: "Is this Mr. Hamilton Fish?" "No," replied Dib. "This is Mr. Tropical Fish."

Learning the Trade

After six months under Bud Watson's command, Phil Newsom called me over and said there was now a place for me on the regular news desk. I would get another raise (all the way up to $27.50) and be placed initially on the afternoon shift—2 to 10 P.M.—working mostly for Arnold Dibble and his assistant editor, Ed Korry, both of whom became lifelong friends.

On the United Press radio desk, incoming news from all over the world was rewritten for the spoken word and dispatched by teletype to 1,400 radio stations across the nation. Radio in those pre-TV days was the source of all instant news. It didn't work to tear a story from the regular news wire and read it over the air. It had to be reworked into shorter sentences and punchy prose and packaged into convenient five- and fifteen-minute segments. These packaged shows would be supplemented by sports and weather stories, feature stories and fillers, usually odd or piquant items useful to fill dead time on a radio show.

Our principal client was the Standard Oil Company of New Jersey, for which we produced "The Esso Reporter." At any hour of the day or night a local disc jockey could pull the latest five-minute news segment from the UP radio wire and intone: "This is your Esso Reporter," and give out with the very latest news. On many stations "The Esso Reporter" was

broadcast every hour on the hour and had to contain fresh elements, all of which kept us very busy indeed. We called these
five-minute shows "WIBs," from "The World in Brief." The fifteen-minute shows were known as roundups. (When my six-
foot-tall friend Lee Jones—"the king-size Rita Hayworth," as
she was affectionately known—and I, five feet two, both
arrived to work one day in our college Persian lamb coats,
someone called out, "Here come the Roundup and the Wib,"
and the names stuck for a while.)

There is a distinct knack to radio news writing, and our
bible was the *UP Radio Style Book,* written by Phil Newsom.
Sentences, for one thing, were shortened for easier delivery.
Successful radio copy had a distinct beat to it; you had to hear
it, not see it. And sibilants were taboo ("Sixteen suicides saw
Stanford staggering" was not a good radio sentence). You had
to be conscious moreover that a listener might tune in at any
moment in the broadcast, which made it necessary to repeat
the name of the person you were writing about more frequently than would be necessary in a regular news story. People were found to be innocent, or guilty. We didn't use "not
guilty" because a listener might turn on his set between the
"not" and the "guilty." That kind of thing. Great attention was
also paid to sensibilities. If one hundred Flying Fortresses went
on a raid and ninety-eight came back, you didn't say "only two
were lost," because some listener's husband, father, son, or
brother might be aboard that missing Fort. You wrote either
"ninety-eight came back," or "two bombers are missing."

A cardinal rule was that when difficult-to-pronounce names
came up, the rewriteman supplied the pronunciation to help
the announcer read it right off without hesitation. The classic

story of what happened when such precautions were omitted is the bulletin filed in the Congo when Dag Hammerskjöld's plane crashed. The first sentence read: "The secretary-general of the United Nations is believed to have been killed in a plane crash in Africa." When one announcer came upon Dag Hammerskjöld's name in the second sentence with no clue as to its pronunciation, he smoothly interjected: "The victim's identity is being withheld pending notification of relatives."

In the early forties, the networks were small and struggling; United Press with its 1,400 client stations was the nation's largest radio news service, which gave us the heady feeling that we were in the front lines of news delivery.

There were, in general, three rewritemen on every shift. When we came in, the editor in charge—George Marder in the morning, Arnold Dibble in the afternoon, Ed Korry often on the overnight—would assign us one of three news areas: the home front, the Western front, and the Pacific. We'd inherit a folder from our predecessor that contained clips of all the incoming stories from the various desks: the foreign news desk, the cable desk, the city desk, the domestic bureaus, and the rest. He'd tell us how much copy—we talked in terms of news minutes—he wanted us to produce. On a hot news day in Europe, the Western front might be assigned eight minutes of the fifteen-minute report, the Pacific two minutes, and the home front five. But these segments could change as the news changed. An editor or a copy boy would keep replenishing our folder with more details, changed casualty figures, new enemy attacks, whatever, and we would have to weave them into our copy.

Often the editor, impatient to put the package together, would come over and tear the paper out of the typewriter as you plugged away. George Marder, unaccustomed to dealing with sensitive young women, once crumpled up Mary Frances Jordan's copy and flung it in her face telling her it WOULD NOT DO. She burst into tears. Poor George was flabbergasted. No one he had ever worked with had burst into tears. Usually they would just swear back at him and attack the story again. Mary Frances wasn't cut out for fast-action news rewrite, but since she was so very nice and sweetly Southern and willing to work practically for free, she was reassigned to the Feature Department to churn out stories for the Sunday supplements. (Features was, in our *collitchgirl* minds, the equivalent of the Woman's Page.)

An Ear and Good Timing

To be good at radio rewrite you had to have an ear, good news sense, and an excellent memory so that you could absorb the news that was bombarding you from all quarters and reshape it in your mind into a coherent story with the numbers falling into place when called for. There was no time to leaf through the mounds of copy and check that it was ninety-eight bombers that got back, not ninety-six. Intelligence helped, but to be able to recognize the news nut and play it hard was essential. Digital dexterity—how fast you could hit those typewriter keys whatever technique you favored—was essential. (Sometimes you had to make an instant judgment call as when, on the night of FDR's death, we got word that Harry S. Truman's first reaction when told he was now president of the United States was, "I felt like as if a load of hay had fallen on my head." After a quick consultation we excised the offending "like.")

Both Lee Jones and Randolph ("Randy") Jennings had those talents, plus intelligence. Lee would go on to become articles editor of *This Week* magazine in its heyday, and later the managing intelligence at Magnum, the premier news photograph agency in the nation. Randy would run UP's West Virginia bureau at Charlestown and later, while her husband Norman Farquhar was going to law school at night in D.C., write most of the famous Eric Severeid fifteen-minute eleven o'clock news show in the early fifties. She wrote the ten-minute news segment, he the prestigious five-minute commentary that led to his later career in television.

Randy spent most of her UP days on the overnight shift, which was just as well. She, a West Virginia friend of hers, named Cissie Lively, who worked for Pan Am, and I once shared an apartment on Forty-seventh Street and Lexington Avenue. We were attracted to it by its wide enclosed wooden balcony on which we had a swinging couch, a picnic table, a cot, and several chairs. We slept there because the apartment had only one small single-bed bedroom. But come winter, when the winds howled through the wooden frame of the porch, we managed with just the bedroom only by working three different shifts: Cissie the conventional day shift, I the 2 to 10 P.M., and Randy the midnight to seven.

It's Bische, Pronounced BEESH

It was Randy who pulled off a truly joyous caper. American forces pushing out from the Ardennes in Belgium were headed for a small but important rail junction at a town called Bische.

Our managers, rightly fearful that when Bische—pronounced Beesh—fell some disc jockey would mispronounce it, ordered us to include its proper pronunciation in caps whenever we mentioned the town. "Attn: Editors: Bische is pronounced B E E S H." To no avail. When the bulletin came in early one morning that Bische had fallen, Randy started her news report: "The sons of Bische surrendered tonight."

In those days if the United Press wire had carried "bitch" or any other off-color word, dozens of newspapers and radio stations in the Southern bible belt would have canceled their contracts instantly. So when, some years later, President Truman blew his stack at *Washington Post* music critic Paul Hume for savaging his daughter Margaret's performance in a concert, the UP reporter handled it thus: President Truman, he said, called the *Post* critic: "a --- -- - ----." Within minutes, a client was complaining that he couldn't figure out what that last four-letter word could be, which occasioned the following deadpan correction: "Correction, In 2nd lead Truman, 2nd pgh, make it read xxx called him "a --- -- - -----.""

On another overnight shift, the cable desk sent out a story about an obscure military action which was datelined "Globasawanne, India." The *New York Times*, then as now insufferably prissy and precise, called demanding that UP pinpoint Globasawanne on the map. Someone sighed and reached for the atlas, and many heads pored over it, magnifying glasses were invoked, but no Globasawanne could be located. It was only then that some old-timer went back to the original cable story and found that Globa Sawanne was the name of the local stringer who had originated the story, not the place from which he was writing.

Datelines sometimes were too good not to be used. Some years later when Bryce Miller was running UP's Saigon bureau he found out that Senator Robert Kennedy would be touring a small village he had spotted in the south called Phuc Binh. When the day came Miller filed the story datelined "Phuc, Vietnam," and to his delight it played throughout Asia. It was only when it got to New York that some spoilsport changed the dateline to Saigon.

On the Sunday that Mussolini and his mistress Clara Petacci were lynched, we news staffers were lunching, not at a quick eatery as usual, but because it was Sunday, and LeRoy Pope, who was handling the desk, was in a permissive mood, at an inexpensive, small Italian restaurant in the East Forties run by a family of former Italian circus aerialists who had taken to pasta. The walls were plastered with pictures of the Flying Carbonari, or whatever was their name, slim, fit, and stern, pulling off impossible feats eighty feet above the sawdust circus floor. But that was all behind them, impossible even to imagine. Now they were a rollicking bunch, friendly and boisterous, each one stouter than the last, and the various spaghetti they served with the cheap Chianti warmed the cockles. Our merriment was cut short when a panting copy boy—one of several who had been dispatched to find us—put his head in the door and summoned us back to handle the biggest news story of the day. We found poor LeRoy, all alone in the slot, doing a magnificent job at fielding the questions, writing the stories, urging the punchers (teletype operators) on, snatching copy from incoming wires, sliding back into his chair fingers flying. It was *collitchgirls* to the rescue! Never was a man happier to see his by-now-veteran staff walk in the door.

War on the Home Front, Joe Panico Commanding

Bibulous, paunchy Joe Panico was an Italian teletype operator, a slam-bang performer both at his keyboard and in the local beer halls, with a sense of humor and total lack of decorum. In these final war years, 1944 and 1945, Joe perfected his rendition of falling bombs. It started with a high whistle and whine, getting louder as it approached the target and ending with a climactic BOOM! that resounded throughout the newsroom. When Joe was on a bombing raid, we, around the corner from the main newsroom in the radio alcove, would often join in the fun. Someone would pick up an oversize stapler, turn it upside down, and slam it together in a clickety-click sound that passed for machine-gun fire. On the other side of the U, people would drop to the floor, pick up discarded sheets of yellow copy paper, roll them into balls, and throw them slowly across the room in high arching arcs, making like grenades, and adding their smaller ca-runch ca-runch to Joe's whining bomb. A rifle squad, armed with rulers, would snake under the desks to ambush the machine-gun nest. Pow, pow, powpowpow! (Bud Watson, needless to say, did not take part.)

Late one evening when the battle was at its peak, Hugh Baillie, then president of United Press, hove round the corner with the president of Standard Oil of New Jersey—UP's single largest radio account—in tow, and spreading his arms expansively, intoned: "This is your Esso Reporter." BOOM! Clickety-click! Ca-runch! Pow! Silence.

The radio desk was formally admonished the following morning to cease and desist from playing war. Joe Panico was

This is your Esso Reporter—
BOOM! Clickety-click! Ca-runch! Pow! Silence!

silenced, not to reappear in full bombing form until the great and glorious VJ-Day.

VJ-Day

VE-Day had been cathartic, but the war was far from over. Veteran troops, brought back from Europe, were in training in the South for the eventual invasion of the Japanese home islands. It was estimated, given the demonstrated fighting spirit of Japanese troops in the stiff Pacific island battles, Iwo Jima, Guadalcanal, Leyte, that the conquest and defeat of the Empire of the Rising Star would cost a million U.S. casualties. This was the compelling rationale for using the atom bomb.

The first rumors that the Japanese might be making overtures about surrender terms through Swiss intermediaries came on Friday, August 11, 1945.

My heart sank. That was the day I was leaving on a precious four-day visit to my sister Aloïse in Falls Church, Virginia. Four-day weekends were not easy to come by, but I had made a deal with Bob Graff, a navy fighter pilot who had been discharged because of injuries when his plane was shot down. Bob was the first veteran to be hired, late in 1944. I would work two days of Bob's shift in one fortnight, and he would work two days of my upcoming shift, which would give us each a four-day weekend in exchange for working ten days in a row. I was longing to see Allie and Ben, and their year-old Jimmy, but I might miss the biggest story of the decade.

Off I went, but I stayed glued to the radio over most of the weekend, monitoring every rumor and wild report about what was going on behind the scenes between Tokyo, Bern, London, and Washington. A second and a third day passed, and still nothing solid had developed. I boarded the train for Pennsylvania Station on the morning of the fourth day in time to report for work on my regular 2 P.M. shift. As I walked in the door it was apparent nothing much was happening, but just minutes later we got the word that Truman, who had become president on Roosevelt's death in April, would speak to the nation at 7 P.M., and in London, Clement Attlee, who had replaced Churchill in July, would speak to the British people at midnight, when BBC ordinarily went off the air.

This was it: the BIG ONE. Arnold Dibble was on the desk. He looked around at the staff and said: "Pitts, you'll handle the roundup, all of it." I would write the first fifteen-minute radio news broadcast on the end of World War II. I have it still, on faded teletype paper. Not world-shaking prose, but competent and comprehensive. The FLASH—"Japan Surrenders"—went out at two seconds after 7 P.M. My fifteen-minute broadcast cleared the line at 7:48 P.M. August 14, 1945.

A Wild Night

It was a wild night in that huge, steaming newsroom on Forty-second Street. Every window that could be opened was, and the breeze sent paper flying around the room. Reporters in Times Square called in their color stories as fast as they could collar a phone and a phone booth quiet enough to dictate from. Dibble had sent a bulletin to every UP radio bureau in the land, ordering them to file two-minute pieces, no more, on celebrations in their area, to come in alphabetically, Albany, Albuquerque, and so on, at a given hour. From this wire, editors all over the country could pick the bits of color they wanted to enliven their report—if it needed any enlivening on that glorious night—and we at NXR (call letters) would stitch whatever stories caught our imagination into our five- and fifteen-minute reports.

There were some lovely ones. A troopship with veterans of the First Division, which had done so much of the heavy fighting in Europe, had left San Diego two days earlier en route to staging areas in the Philippines where they would train for the invasion of the Japanese homeland. As the veterans listened to news of the surrender, the ship made a 180-degree turn, and headed back to San Diego. Silence, followed by a tumultuous roar.

Off the Japanese coast the Third Fleet was on patrol. Admiral Bull Halsey announced the end of the war to his command but added: "Should any hostile plane fly overhead shoot it down in friendly fashion."

Punchers and rewritemen didn't even try to conceal the huge cartons of beer they carried in from the local saloons—no one would interfere with the open breach of the no-drinking rule on this night of nights. The overnight shift arrived but the night shift refused to leave. It was too much fun. It was too great. We—with the help of a few million soldiers, sailors, marines, and airmen—had done it, we had brought Hirohito and his war machine to their knees.

Mary Frances and Ensign Raffles

We were starting to receive lists of American prisoners of war, men mostly long since given up for dead. Many of these missing-in-action men were carrier pilots who had disappeared into the waters of the vast Pacific. But with the war winding down specially trained army units were being dropped at known POW camps to rescue the survivors lest fanatic Japanese commanders order their execution. The dead were rising from the grave.

Talk of human interest. Mary Frances, the Southern girl whom George Marder had terrified, now happily ensconced in Features, started to haunt the cable desk. Her concern was for Ensign Peter Raffles (I believe that was his name) to whom she had become engaged three years earlier in Memphis. They had been engaged less than a week when he got his orders to join a carrier in the Pacific. Months later, shortly after she arrived at UP, he had been reported missing in action somewhere in the South Pacific. Sometime later she received word from his family that his status had been changed to "presumed dead." That had been eighteen months earlier.

Someone spotted the name on the overnight. There it was, Lieutenant jg Peter Raffles, on a list of rescued prisoners. Love, moon, croon, and June were all very well, but Mary Frances was worried. She had no idea whether she still, or had ever really, loved Peter. The courtship had been such a heady, whirlwind affair, a class graduating from flight school, awaiting orders. Like so many others in those frantic days, Mary Frances and Peter got engaged and off he went to battle.

In due course there was a phone call from a hospital in California: it was Peter. Mary Frances applied for a leave and left by train, the only way to travel those days, for the uncomfortable four-day ride across the country to meet a man she realized she hardly knew. That was the last we ever saw of Mary Frances. She and Peter were married and for years I would receive a Christmas card with a photo of Peter and Mary Frances, Peter, Mary Frances, and Joey, Peter, Mary Frances, Joey, and Mary Lou, and on until one day they stopped coming, and it was a year or so later before I noticed the omission, as tends to happen with friends whose paths you no longer cross.

Old Friend and Good

Rita Meyer and I overlapped at UP for only a few months. Rita was definitely not a *collitchgirl*; she had come up the hard way, working on small dailies, finally landing a job at UP in her late twenties or early thirties. Her husband was in the Coast Guard where, according to Rita, he spent most of his time playing

A visit to the ruins of Angkor Wat

chess by long-distance telephone. One gathered that they were not close. Rita moved on after a few months and disappeared from our ken.

In 1961 I was in Thailand with my mother, my brother Jim, and his wife Ann. Jim was then exploring for oil in the Philippines. We had just returned to Bangkok after a glorious four-day visit to the ruins of Angkor Wat, which would very shortly after be shut off from the world when Pol Pot went about his vision of a new, and terrorized, Khmer Rouge civilization.

Mother had a bad cold, which was getting worse, not better, and I feared for her on the next day's scheduled long flight home, via Hawaii. An American I sat next to at a lunch that my friend Jim Burnham had arranged suggested that I call a Dr. Jacobson, a Danish doctor who had a clinic just outside the city. Dr. Jacobson was most accommodating, said my new friend, and would either make a call on Mother or see her at his clinic. Back at the hotel I called the number, and was relieved when the woman who answered spoke English. I told her my story. She asked for the name of the patient. Mrs. William F. Buckley Sr. "I don't suppose she's related to Priscilla Buckley," said the voice on the other end. "This is Priscilla Buckley," I said. "Well, sonovagun. Hi, Pitts, this is Rita Meyer from UP." The husky drawl was unmistakable. It was indeed my old friend Rita, who was now—seventeen years later—Mrs. Dr. Jacobson.

Her story was a lulu. After the war she had taken a job as a public relations spokesman for the then reigning Thai government. Three days after her arrival in Bangkok a palace coup had sent Rita's employers into exile or jail. In the ensuing roundup of political undesirables, Rita was plucked from her new office and plunked into prison, and there she stayed for three months before the American Embassy managed to get her released. It was while recuperating from that experience—Thai jails were (and are) anything but spas—that she had met Dr. Jacobson.

The doctor called on Mother that afternoon, gave her a shot, and assured me that it would be safe for her to fly home.

The Music Man

Johnny Zischaung, like Rita and so many journeyman newsmen in those days, was a rolling stone. Johnny had been born with a stump instead of a left hand. He was short, with thinning reddish hair, quiet, and very shy. He did his work well, but without enthusiasm. He was hard to get to know, on the defensive in personal relations. It was only in his cups that Johnny came to life. He played a mean piano despite his disability, hitting a steady bass with the stump of his left hand while his right hand moved with astonishing agility over the usually tinny keyboard of the uprights to be found in many Greenwich Village apartments. He wrote songs and was the beery life of many an impromptu postwork party in the Village where most of us lived in dirty, crowded, cramped apartments. One of Johnny's songs I remember—I can almost hear the thump-thump of its beat today—was entitled "The Blonde and the Yokel on the Uptown Local."

Johnny and I became friends and then buddies because one Wednesday when he was broke he touched me for a five-dollar loan to tide him over to payday (if what we received from UP can be called such) on Friday. When I came to work that Friday, Johnny was there five bucks in hand. That set a pattern. I ended up keeping the five dollars in a separate compartment in my purse, lest I inadvertently spend it, to lend to Johnny every Wednesday. I got it back every Friday. Like clockwork. It became our joke. "Pitts is always borrowing from me," Johnny would remark as he ostentatiously gave me back my bill on Friday. Improvident Johnny was, but not a cadger.

No one liked Johnny's then wife. Her name, I think, was Betty, and our dislike was reinforced by an incident at a party in the Village one night. The Zischaungs were temporarily quartered in Margaret's apartment. Margaret was our unit's Guild representative and in that capacity had heard that the Zischaungs had been evicted from their apartment, probably for nonpayment of rent. She kindly offered them her own place for the three weeks she would be out of town on assignment. That would give them a breathing space to find new digs. We were all there one night, clustered around the piano, when Betty came into the living room with a shoebox full of letters. She had found it tucked away on the top shelf of the closet, way back supposedly out of reach.

"Look what I've found," she said with glee, and proceeded to read a juicy segment from a love letter to Margaret from her lesbian partner, a phys ed teacher at Smith College. "Cut it out," said Johnny from the piano, stern for once. "Betty, put those letters back." She did, albeit reluctantly. Some of us, Margaret's friends, left, thanking Johnny, but ignoring Betty, furious at her betrayal of Margaret's confidence and kindness.

I was relieved that Margaret's friend was not my particular favorite Smith phys ed teacher. My friend was tall, slim, and attractive with the brightest smiling light blue eyes. She had been the coach of our all-Smith golf team and had frequently piled two or three girls into the front seat of her rickety mid-thirties Chevy convertible, our clubs in the light canvas bags we carried in those days rattling around in the rumble seat, and driven us to the Mt. Tom golf course in Holyoke where we practiced and played our matches. Once, made jubilant by our unexpected victory over a faculty team headed by Smith President Jonathan Davies, she had even stopped en route home at a local tavern and bought us each an illicit beer.

After I left UP, Johnny moved over to the nascent television division, did well, and ended up years later as Paris TV manager. (This was after I had returned to New York from Paris.) I heard of his tragic death from Robert Ahier, a great buddy of mine in my UP Paris days. Johnny had fallen into the Seine one night and drowned, the exact circumstances of his death unclear. His host of friends suspected he had had a cup too many as on so many evenings past and hoped the fatal stumble had followed a rousing rendition of whatever was

Johnny's current "The Blonde and the Yokel on the Uptown Local."

War's Over

The war was over, and, as promised, veterans were returning to claim the civilian jobs they had left to go to war. Despite the waiver all the *collitchgirls* had signed agreeing to resign when the boys came home, no one was asked to leave. (I learned many years later that virtually every woman hired by AP during the war had been given the heave-ho as soon as they could be replaced.) The former servicemen hired on the radio news desk were all newcomers to UP. Each had a story. Bob Graff, the first returnee, had been so badly burned when his plane was shot down that while the surgeons had done a magnificent job in giving him a new face, it turned out to be so different from his old face that his mother had not recognized him at first. Bob went on to become a bigwig at NBC.

Dick Witkin, a bombardier in the European theater, was wiry, dark, intense, with a slight nervous tic. He didn't do much talking about the war. He was friendly in a quiet, withdrawn way in contrast to his bubbling dancer wife Kate who would shortly land a part in the chorus line of the newest Broadway hit, *Call Me Mister*. A bunch of us were in the audience on opening night to cheer Katie's performance. Dick went on to become the *New York Times* transportation editor and covered most of the Cape Canaveral space stories, including the Apollo 11 launch. When you became a friend of Dick Witkin's you were a friend for life. He was one of my particular favorites.

Marvin Lorber's Story

Marvin Lorber was everything Dick Witkin was not. Also a flier, he loped around the newsroom in long, easy strides, amused by every little happening, a smile always at the ready. He was the epitome of relaxedness in a frenzied environment, unflappable, a pleasant companion at work or play. He had spent a couple of years in a prisoner-of-war camp in Romania, after being shot down on a strike at the Ploesti oil fields. One night, over a sandwich and a pitcher of beer at the Old Brew House on Fifty-third Street, he told me his story. It had Marvin's characteristic ironic spin. The first big American raid on the Ploesti oil fields that were vital to the Nazi war machine was flown from a base near Benghazi. A cocky flyboy brigadier general led the raid and when they were returning to base he broke radio silence to proclaim: "I saw Ploesti die tonight."

Six months later in yet another raid on the far-from-dead Ploesti field, Marvin Lorber's bomber was shot down. He parachuted out and was almost immediately picked up by a Romanian army patrol. On arriving at the prison camp he was put in a barracks with other captured American fliers where he joined their elite club which was called "The I Saw Ploesti Die Tonight Club," membership limited to those who had been on that original raid, as Marvin had.

Conditions in the camp at the end of the war were frightful, Marvin went on. But the lot of the American and British prisoners, cold and hungry as they were, was nothing compared to that of the Russians, who were abused, tortured, kicked, and starved. The camp commander was a dandy, a lipsticked homosexual, always exquisitely turned out, and a sadist. He enjoyed ordering men stripped, flogged, and shot. Toward the end, as the Nazi war machine crumbled and the Red Army moved into Romania, conditions in the camp worsened dramatically. The officers in the British-American barracks knew from the clandestine radio they had pieced together that Romania was about to fall. The end came very suddenly. There was a frenzied knocking at the barracks door on a bleak winter's night. It was the commandant, white with fear. The Russian prisoners had burst out of their barracks on news that the Red Army was at the gates, intent on revenge. The prison guards had fled, and the Russians were after the commandant. He pled with the Americans and British to give him sanctuary. Marvin paused, his easy flow interrupted by the memories of that moment. He was not smiling. "What did you do?" I couldn't stand the suspense. "We threw the bastard out . . ."

"And?"

"And they tore him to pieces."

Home Is the Sailor

The call was for me, which was unusual. We got very few personal calls at United Press, partially at least because no one had a desk and his own telephone. The connection was so fuzzy that Phil Newsom had it transferred to his phone where the background din was less obtrusive, and motioned me to his chair.

It was Jimmy, brother Jim, on a very bad line, calling from San Diego. He was back in the States after two and a half years in the South Pacific aboard LST (landing ship tanks) *1013*. And he had gotten his discharge that morning. He would get whatever transportation he could and would probably be in New York in three or four days. What he wanted was to surprise Mother.

So we arranged it. He would come to the UP office when he arrived, and he and I would drive home to Sharon in time for supper. I burbled that his timing was superb. Everyone, but everyone, was home, or would be home by the weekend. Our oldest sister Aloïse, her husband Ben Heath, and little Jimmy were in Sharon, Connecticut, while Ben decided what he would do next. He had been discharged as a major in the Army Air Corps. John, next in line to Aloïse, was back from France, finishing the dissertation he still owed Yale before he could claim his diploma. He had volunteered for service halfway through his senior year, right after Peal Harbor. And Bill, number six, was in Sharon, freshly discharged from an infantry camp in Texas where he had been stationed for the last few months.

Jim and I would drive out in my new car, a tiny Plymouth two-door sedan. The connection was too bad for me to explain how come I owned a car, but I would tell Jimmy all about it on the hundred-mile drive north from New York to Sharon, where all ten of us had been brought up in a rambling old clapboard house just off the town green.

At one time when his oldest four—Aloïse, John, Jim, and I—were in college, Father had told us that "in the unlikely event" that any one of us could save enough money to buy half a car, he would pay for the other half. Dear Father, a spendthrift himself, was always trying to instill habits of frugality in his children, with signal lack of success.

A car was what I wanted most in life, the only large object I had ever coveted, so I had gotten into the habit on payday, which was Friday, of going to the bank on the ground floor of the Daily News Building and putting whatever change was left in my purse from last week's salary—$1.62, $2.45, 87 cents, whatever—into a savings account, while cashing the current check. I had also put my name in for a new Plymouth with dear old Mr. Benjamin in Winsted, Connecticut, from whom Father had bought cars for a number of years. There would be a long waiting list for new cars after the wartime drought, I knew. In due course my little hoard hit the magic $600 mark—you could buy a (modest) new car in 1946 for $1,200—and when Mr. Benjamin called one day out of the blue to say my car was on the lot, a much surprised Father dutifully ponied up the additional $600.

I had no trouble arranging my schedule for Jim's arrival with Arnold Dibble, who was in charge of day-to-day activities on the radio desk. I could take whatever afternoon I wanted off, he said. He'd just call someone else in to take my place. This was the kind of thing that kept people at United Press. Whereas the front office was brutal in its handling of staff, the people you actually worked for, the Newsoms and Dibbles and Marders, and later on the Korrys and Millers and Landreys and Higbees in Paris, understood the importance of a brother's return from an active zone of war.

Two or three days later, in walked a skinny bronzed young man in a rumpled grey uniform and the smile that had mesmerized me since the next toddler in line first turned it on me. I had last seen him in mid-1944, the night before he sailed. We had taken in the final night of A Connecticut Yankee at King Arthur's Court, and afterward had a farewell brandy Alexander at Longchamps.

I phoned Sharon to let Aloïse know we were on our way.

She said she would try to delay supper until we arrived. We drove across town, through the Garment District, and up the West Side Drive. Anchored in the Hudson were elements of the Pacific Fleet on a postwar victory tour of major U.S. ports. I had written a series of two- and three-minute profiles of the more famous ships, those massive grey silhouettes in the sun-bespeckled waters of the Hudson. Jim had taken part in three Pacific island invasions, including Okinawa and Leyte, but he had never seen a giant flattop until I pointed the *Endeavor* out to him on that sunny, happy drive along the Hudson.

Buckleys were chockablock around the big table in the dining room, with Mother as usual perched on the massive chair at the head of the table, one leg tucked under the other, and Father, at the foot. As we walked in there was just an instant of silence and then Mother was on her feet: "Jimmy . . . Jimmy," and running to meet and hug him. Then everyone was up, pounding backs, embracing, kissing. And the little children, who had been finishing their supper at the middle table, were all over Jim, only little Carol hanging back. She had been four when last she saw him, and now she was seven. Ella managed, in all the commotion, to set another place at Mother's right, and everyone was asking Jim what his war had been like, but all he wanted to do was find out what we had been up to in his absence. Every once in a while Mother would reach out and take his hand, so happy to have him here, and we would smile at each other because it was well known in the family that Jimmy was Mother's favorite—and such is Jim's diffidence that no one ever minded the fact.

Mother interrupted the general babble. "Will, dear," she said, "we *must* call Miss Sipprell *tomorrow*, now that all the boys are home." Miss Clara Sipprell took family pictures that came out wispy and slightly Victorian in flavor and always, it seemed to me, just the slightest bit out of focus. But Mother and Father thought they were grand. The boys, as a man, announced that they would *not* be photographed in their uniforms: that that uniform stuff, and saluting and such, was behind them, old history.

But at lunch on Saturday, when Jeff told Mother that Miss Sipprell had set up her camera and that he had brought a bench out and placed it, at her instructions, in front of the Great Elm, Mother ordered the boys to "run upstairs and get dressed," as if they were still five-year-olds, and without a word, the airman, the two soldiers, and the sailor disappeared to reappear fifteen minutes later in uniform, Jim's navy blues now cleaned and pressed.

The black-and-white photograph still stands in its battered red leather frame in the patio, with little Jimmy Heath sitting stiff-legged on the bench between his mother and grandmother, the girls, Jane, Patricia, Maureen, Carol, and I, in short-sleeved summer dresses, Ben, John, Jim, and Bill in uniform, and off to the right, just a bit removed, sixteen-year-old Reid in a linen jacket and khaki slacks looking a mite sullen. The only thing wrong with World War II, in Reid's opinion, was that it had ended before he was old enough to join in the fracas.

Moving On

After the War, a restlessness settled on the group that had worked so well together for better than two years. Today's news stories lacked the dramatic excitement of yesterday's. Some of us started to move on. Bobby Ober, the copygirl I had met that first day in 1944, and whose unflappable good humor kept us all laughing a great deal of the time, got a job on a radio station in New Jersey, the second step in a career that would lead her to a protracted stint as executive editor of *Cosmopolitan* under Helen Gurley Brown. Randy Jennings, briefly, very briefly, engaged to Ed Korry, transferred to the Charlestown, West Virginia, bureau when their engagement collapsed. She wanted to be close to her childhood home and her ailing mother. And Ed got himself reassigned to the London bureau. Ed Korry would go on to run UP bureaus in Belgrade and Paris, and become foreign editor of *Look* magazine. He volunteered to write foreign policy speeches for JFK in the 1960 campaign and a thankful President Kennedy appointed him ambassador to Ethiopia. Later he served as ambassador to Chile under Richard Nixon in the tumultuous Frei-Allende years. Lee Jones moved on to *This Week* and later to Magnum, the prestigious photography agency. Dick Amper—who had greeted me the first day when I reported for work—became Governor Nelson Rockfeller's press secretary.

Leroy Pope, who had so feared the advent of the collitch-girls, stayed on at UP and became a noted figure among New York financial and business reporters. He had an encyclopedic memory and a thousand unwritten stories in his head, stories to be tracked down and written up as fast as he could get to them. When computers spelled the doom of the teletype machine and the phasing out of the punchers who had serviced them—Joe Panico and his pals—when the hum of computers replaced the bells and clatter and clamor of the old-time newsroom, Leroy Pope, once again, resisted change. He kept pecking away at his balky old upright Royal and prevailed against the tide of modernity. In his corner of the newsroom one teletype machine and one puncher were retained to send out LeRoy's copy. LeRoy finally retired, age eighty, as UPI headed into a near-terminal tailspin, a trouper to the last, much missed, among others, by a generation of admiring collitchgirls he had taken the time and trouble to hammer into shape.

Oops!

Many of my good friends had left but I was still on hand on that memorable day in 1946 when the Nazi Nuremberg war criminals were to hang. We were waiting for the FLASH that the executions were taking place when, to our astonishment, in came the big brass from the thirteenth floor, superannuated newsmen turned businessmen and number crunchers: They moved in on the news operation and announced that THIS story was so big, THEY would handle it themselves.

The FLASH came. It was unexpected. The head honcho bent over his typewriter and produced a bulletin for the ages. He wrote: "Herman Goering cheated death by committing suicide."

They left as quickly as they had arrived and someone corrected the bulletin to read: "Herman Goering cheated death *by hanging* by committing suicide." How we underlings did laugh. This was a story that would go down in UP underground history along with *The Kansas City Milkman*.

I didn't hear of *The Kansas City Milkman* until I joined the UP bureau in Paris some years later, and someone passed me a crumbling, much-taped-together paperback version of the story, a wickedly hilarious novel on how United Press really worked by longtime Unipresser Reynolds Packard. Everyone in the European division was warned not to read it on pain of dismissal. The title came from the legendary note an early editor had placed on a UP news spike instructing everyone to write stories so simply that the Kansas City milkman could understand them. But that's another tale, for another day.

(((PART TWO)))

PARIS

1953-1956

SO HERE I WAS IN PARIS. It might not have been the best of times, or the worst of times, but it was surely the coldest of times. An icy blast had descended over northern Europe and there it stayed for six solid weeks that winter of 1953. The skies were grey and filled with moisture, freezing rain, and sleet. Slabs of ice floated on the Seine; the City of Light was wrapped in gloom and the suffering was intense. Every morning police would find frozen corpses under the bridges of Paris. Suddenly everyone was talking about l'Abbé Pierre, that bearded angel of mercy who seemed to be everywhere, picking up the derelicts, feeding them hot potage and bread, binding up their wounds, finding shelter for them.

It was cold, too, in the tiny garret maid's room I was occupying under the eaves of the Hôtel France et Choiseul on the Rue St. Honoré. The charge for these minimalist quarters was $8 a day, for which you got a cot, a chair, a small table, a washbasin, but also breakfast. The bathtub and toilet were down the hall. The bath was an extra dollar and had to be ordered en route up.

I had been hired to work at United Press in Paris and my conditioned reflex from earlier experience with UP had kicked in. The message received was loud and clear: keep expenses down. I would stay at the France et Choiseul until I could find a reasonably inexpensive apartment in a Paris still working its way back from the ravages of the war.

Supper with Ed Korry

My new venture had come about pretty much by accident. Earlier this year I had been in Washington, working at the CIA in one of those depressing World War I temporary buildings hard by the Lincoln Memorial. The phone rang. It was Ed Korry, my old friend from United Press days in New York five or six years earlier. Ed was now Paris bureau manager of UP and in Washington to cover a high-level meeting between French Foreign Minister Antoine Pinay and Secretary of State John Foster Dulles. This was 1953 and the Western nations were stitching together a series of treaties that would bring the war to a formal end and establish the international bodies— NATO, the European Steel and Coal Community, the Parliament of Europe—that would shape the postwar, cold war–dominated world.

Ed was free that night. Pinay was at a private dinner at the French Embassy, so the two of us went out for supper. It was a pleasant evening. We reminisced for a few minutes about old friends, where they were, what they were up to. I was happy to see Ed again, and to listen to his stories. He had been in Belgrade, and had become an unexpected favorite of Marshal

Tito because he had coached a local basketball team that had gone on to win an international tournament. Ed had been the only Western correspondent to get into the show trial of Cardinal Mindszenty in Hungary. His life sounded wonderfully exciting. Mine at CIA at this point was pretty much paper-pushing, and if I put in for an overseas post the chances were that I would end up in Frankfurt, a prospect that thrilled me not at all.

Halfway through the evening, Ed said, casually, that if I would like to work for UP in Paris, it could be easily arranged. There were seven staffers on the American desk in the Paris bureau and the turnover—given UP salaries and the six-day week the overseas bureaus worked—was rapid. If I was serious about the job, he said, I should let him know, then go to Europe and maybe do a bit of traveling while awaiting the next opening. It might be a month, but probably no longer.

I accepted then and there. There's an excitement about raw news that is hard to explain, but it is palpable, and once you are bitten by the news bug, nothing else seems quite so stimulating.

2 Rue des Italiens

Tomorrow I would report for work, but not to Ed Korry, it seemed, because Ed was in Geneva covering an important international meeting. He had left a letter for me at the hotel telling me to report to Ken Miller, who was the news editor and second in command of the Paris bureau. Ken Miller had left a telephone message telling me to see him at 10 A.M., which would give him time to get the morning news report going.

The UP bureau was just off the Boulevard des Italiens, on the opposite side of the Opéra from La Madeleine. We were at 2 Rue des Italiens, a small block-long side street off the boulevard. It took a sharp turn halfway down, where a building housed *Le Monde*, France's equivalent of the *New York Times*. *Le Monde* was sturdily leftist and a good deal greyer even than the *Times*. In those days it carried no pictures on its front page. There was no question, however, but that its editors and writers ate better than those at the *Times*. They could be spotted most noons at Le Petit Riche on Rue le Peletier tucking in enormous three-course lunches.

Our stout six- or seven-story building had seen better days. On the ground floor on the right was a cheesy small photography shop whose owner, M. Michel, was also our local black-market currency dealer. No one, but no one, at that time changed money at the legal rate of approximately 350 old francs to the dollar. M. Michel gave us eight points under the rate quoted in the morning Paris *Herald Tribune*, a reasonable exchange. On the left as you entered the building you went down two or three steps into a low-class Corsican nightclub. The glassed-in elevator in the center of the hall, by the winding stairwell, was encased in a cloak of wrought iron and had once been very elegant. It rose particularly slowly.

In that elevator that first morning I learned a lesson about the French. I had entered the elevator with two men in heavy overcoats, scarves, gloves, and hats. "Good morning," I had remarked. "It's cold." One of them nodded: "*Il ne fait pas chaud*," he commented. ("It's not warm.") One doesn't say it's cold, one says it's not warm, that's the way the French approach so many subjects: obliquely. Lesson one.

I stepped off on the fourth floor, as instructed, and hesitated before pushing open the tall, double French doors.

The clatter was familiar, just as of old. Typewriters and teletype machines going great guns, phones ringing, men calling to each other across lines of desks and typewriters. Sitting in the slot was Ken Miller. His greeting was not hostile, but it was less than warm, totally polite and yet I knew at once that something was bugging him and I feared that it was me, the fact of me.

Could it be because I was a woman? There were no women on the American desk although women were sprinkled about the large newsroom, which also accommodated the far larger French desk. As I was to find out later, after Ken and I had become friends, it was indeed my sex that was causing the trouble, but not in the way I thought. Ken wasn't a chauvinist. The problem was that he feared that I would want to cover the French fashion scene, and most particularly cover the spring and fall collections of the great fashion houses: Dior, Givenchy, Chanel, Nina Ricci, and the rest.

This assignment had been handled by Ken's wife Barbara for the last year and the Millers feared that with a woman on the staff United Press would expect her to cover fashions, thus saving Barbara's (modest, very) stipend. After someone tipped me off, I assured Ken that I didn't know a seam from a gusset, and had no interest in learning. Shades of the Woman's Page I had spent my earlier UP career avoiding.

For the first couple of weeks Ken assigned me to the 10 A.M. to 7 P.M. shift so that he could keep an eye on me and gauge my competence. I met the other American desk staffers who were also suspending judgment until they had seen me in action. This was a totally different situation from the UP radio desk where I had broken in to newspaper work, with the added imponderable: how good was my French and how serviceable my vocabulary? I didn't really know.

My Colleagues

It was a mixed cast of characters, those initial colleagues of mine at 2 Rue des Italiens. Nick King, who would become my dearest friend, was on the corpulent side, a fine figure of a man, as a Victorian novelist might have described him: tall, six foot-two or three, erudite, slow moving and slow speaking, a scholar and a gentleman, a first-class newspaperman and a classy human being. His prose sang when given the chance. When he died of a massive stroke in the mid 1990s—I had had lunch with him the day before—the *Wall Street Journal* paid him a unique tribute: they made room for four separate pieces by him, two travel articles, a book review, and an essay on manners and civility, on their Op-Ed page the following day. It was the last word in professional courtesy, a gesture Nick would have appreciated.

Bob Rigby was a good-looking Midwesterner in his early thirties with an enchanting Norwegian artist wife, Amy, and two tiny boys, Leif and Michael. I would spend two Christmases and a wondrous holiday in Bordeaux with the Rigbys in the next couple of years, and if not otherwise engaged often spent my day off with them in their tiny little house in Le Vésinet, a pleasant suburb.

Danny Halperin, who was generally on the overnight shift,

was a Canadian and we suspected a remittance man. There was a mystery in Danny's past; he never ever spoke of it and evaded all questions about his life prior to Paris. Danny was compulsively neat even when he grew a luxuriant beard, which he did every time he was posted for a month or more to the overnight shift. Neatness was a mania with Danny; he couldn't even bear a messy "spike."

The spike is the record of the day's news operations. As soon as a "take" on any outgoing story was written, a copy of it was put on spike. During the day the spike was a hodgepodge of papers impaled on it at every which angle. But whoever relieved Danny at 7 A.M. would find all of the items on the spike neatly aligned with their edges cut by Danny's big scissors so that no one sheet of paper hung over the edge of another one. Everything that had been written and punched out on the teletype would appear on the spike—the story, the corrections, the updates, the inserts. It was placed to the right of the slot within easy reach of the editor. The first thing you did when reporting for work was pull a chair up to the desk and read the spike to get a running picture of what was the big news of the moment, what stories were ongoing, what needed to be done. An editor might leave a note for an incoming staffer to remind him to pick up on a given story, or instructing him to meet someone at such and such a time for an interview.

Everything appears on the spike—the story, the corrections, the updates, the inserts.

It was the thread that kept us all on the track. It was important only to Danny that the spike be not only informative but neat.

There were almost as many non-Americans as Americans on the so-called American desk. Jack Schmeil, whose mother was French and father Egyptian, was in the office irregularly. He covered society events, the Cannes film festival, visiting celebrities, international playboys, all that was glitzy. He wasn't really part of the working team, which is to say that things would have to get very tight indeed before anyone would leave Jack in the slot, which is the nerve center of the news operation. Schmeil made every effort to keep his distance. The idea of being a journeyman correspondent held no appeal for him. Robert Ahier, dear, silly, conceited, noisy, insecure Bob Ahier, the only Frenchman on the American desk, covered sports and other less serious entertainments. His English prose, of which he was inordinately proud, was the despair of whatever poor soul was on the desk when Bob Ahier filed a story. Accuracy was not a word he understood, or a goal he pursued. He got us into terrible troubles, about which more anon. But he was so good-hearted, so jolly, so obliging, so see-through-able that no one could stay mad at him for long. Some of us never even got mad at him in the first place. In addition, he and Jack covered a lot of the stories—chasing after film stars and oil-rich Arab sheiks—the rest of us would have had to handle had they not been available.

George Sibera's Escape

The class of the non-American American team was George Sibera, whose principal beat was the French parliament. This was during the final years of the Fourth Republic, when government followed government like horses on a merry-go-round, rising and falling every four or five months. The parliamentary shenanigans and Machiavellian intrigues in the Palais Bourbon, where the Chamber of Deputies met, were awesome to behold, almost impossible to explain to a rational world. But George Sibera was up to the job.

George was not French. He was Czech, a remarkable man whose intelligence was matched by his integrity. Five years earlier he had not spoken a word of French or English. He now wrote fluently and even idiomatically in both languages. His was a most remarkable story, but by no means unique in a Europe truncated by Stalin's Iron Curtain.

George was a boy when the Nazis marched into Czechoslovakia in 1938. Ten years later he was in his final year at the University of Prague law school, and head of the Young Socialists at the university. One afternoon his older brother, who was a clerk in the Interior Ministry, called. He was extremely agitated. It was a day or so after Jan Masaryk had been found on the ground outside his office. Masaryk had jumped, or possibly been pushed, to his death out of a third-story window. George must get out of the country at once, that very day. The Communists had prepared a coup and today was the day they would make their move. The brother had come across George's name on a list of those to be arrested in the first sweep of political undesirables. As head of the Young Socialists, he was on the Communist blacklist. Don't wait for anything, the brother implored George, you've got to go now. It's now or never.

George returned to his room in the dorm to pack a few

things. His roommate, who was French, was in. George told him what had happened and the roommate insisted that he take his—the roommate's—passport with which he might be able to board a train to Vienna, and from there to the free West. The roommate, his name was Paul, also insisted that George take whatever cash he had on hand. I'll be all right, he said, I'm French. They won't dare do anything worse than expel me from the country. They embraced, and George left.

The roommate was tall and dark. George was short, five feet six or so, with a broad Slavic face, short reddish-bronze hair, and a huge mole on his right cheek. The passport got George out of the country without difficulty. The Communists had not had time to tighten all the screws. Only once did anyone inspect the picture on the passport carefully, George said, and that was when the train passed over from the Soviet zone in still-occupied Vienna to the Western zone. There a brawny American MP looked at the picture, looked at George, looked back at the picture, and once again at George. Then he smiled, and waved him through. News of the Communist takeover of Czechoslovakia was blaring over the loudspeakers in the station, and that particular GI wasn't going to stop anyone who wanted out.

George Sibera arrived in Paris, twenty-six years old, penniless, and not speaking a word of French. His papers were irregular in the extreme. So he went to work as a dishwasher in a restaurant where no language skills were required and set himself to learning French. He was lucky enough to find a room with a French woman who understood his situation and didn't worry if he was a few days late with the rent. That was his first bit of good luck in a long time. George figured that he wouldn't make it in the French economy. French authorities recognized the rights of asylum, but that was about all they were willing to do for political refugees. So George started to look for work with a foreign firm, preferably an American one. A year or so later, his French now excellent, George spotted an ad for a messenger boy at United Press. One job requirement was that the messenger own a bicycle on which to get around the city. Once again, the kindly landlady came to George's rescue, lending him the money to get the bike. And so George got his toehold with a leading American news agency. While running errands, George also studied English.

All this had been two or three years before my arrival in Paris. By my time, George was acknowledged by all to know more about how the French government worked than anyone else on the staff, American or French.

He had married a charming Frenchwoman, Simone, and they had two small children. But his salary was still minute and he was forced to moonlight with Radio Free Europe to make ends meet. (This was on top of a forty-eight- and often sixty-hour week.) Nothing Ed Korry or subsequent bureau managers would do could get George a raise from a management that pinched every little franc. (My immediate predecessor, Otto Friedrich, had walked out when he had asked for a raise, pointing out that in Paris a box of Kleenex cost a dollar, and Mr. Bradley, the European manager, had replied: "Why do you need Kleenex?" before turning him down cold. Otto was extraordinarily talented, an exceptionally bright journalist who later wrote possibly the best, and certainly the most readable book ever written on pre-Hitler Berlin, *Before the Deluge*. His distinguished career included a stint as the last editor of *The Saturday Evening Post*.)

Among George's regular assignments was coverage of the annual meeting of the Council of Europe in Strasbourg every fall. It was there, sipping a beer at a sidewalk café one evening in the early 1960s, that George spotted a group of four passing by, an older and a younger couple. He jumped up from the table and embraced the surprised younger man. It was Paul, the roommate who had made George's escape from Prague possible so many years earlier. They had not communicated since that day, George fearing that any attempt to get in touch would make things worse for Paul.

The French Empire's Our Beat, All of It

The seven of us on the American desk plus Ken Miller and Ed Korry who was, however, seldom there, ran the office around the clock seven days a week, closing only for seven hours from Sunday midnight to 7 A.M. on Monday. Our beat was the entire French empire: Indochina, then in the climactic stage of its war of independence from France, Equatorial Africa, French North Africa, Morocco, Tunisia, and Algeria, plus its former spheres of influence in the Middle East, Lebanon and Syria, where French interests were still well entrenched. We gathered all the news from these areas, mostly through stringers and careful monitoring of the Agence France-Presse wire and the French press. We translated and rewrote these stories for the international English-language wire that went from Paris to London and then by cable—the Bouverie line—to New York where it was processed and sent out to the rest of the world.

The larger unit that manned the French desk, on the other side of the room, did the reverse. It took the incoming international wire and rewrote the stories of interest to the French press in French. There was little similarity in the French and English versions of the same story. Back in those days we adhered to the who, where, when, why, and how, while a French news story tended to be a delicate piece of embroidery with tantalizing asides, historical references, and a distinct point of view.

Ken Miller

We also went out on assignment, but most of us were tied pretty closely to Paris because, shorthanded as we were, every one of us put in time just keeping the news desk running.

Ken Miller took his job very seriously. His father, Webb Miller, had been somewhat of a UP hero in the flamboyant post–World War I era of enterprising journalists like Richard Halliburton, Lowell Thomas, Dorothy Thompson, and others. Ken desperately wanted to make his mark but he lacked the pizzazz that had made Webb such an enterprising reporter. He was a workhorse, not a showhorse, and endowed with the kind of mental and digital dexterity that UP's autocrats prized highly. He was likable, but just a bit on the pompous side, and he tended to be autocratic. He would seldom reprove you in person, but he could leave scalding notes in a mailbox or worse yet on the spike for all to see. The rest of us were not above gentle retaliations as when Ken incautiously left the following note on the spike: "If General de Castries [the just released

Dien Bien Phu commander] calls I will talk to him *day or night*." Someone inserted, "if General de Castries *or the Pope* . . ."

Ken left himself open for a good deal of not altogether unkind ribbing. He liked to dominate his typewriter, leaning over to hit the keys from high above it. First thing in the morning he would reach over and put three thick volumes on his typewriter chair: usually *Jane's Fighting Ships*, the "P" volume of the 1924 *Encyclopedia Britannica*, and a thick French travel guide to Indochina, circa 1936, that Nick King had picked up on the quais and which provided us with exciting local color with which to embellish our Indochina copy. These raised Ken's rump high in the air. He typed, his head swinging back and forth like a famous Czech track star. He was a veritable "*Zapotek du clavier* [keyboard]," laughed the French punchers. It became a game for a staffer in a teasing mood to say, "I'm sorry, Ken, but I've got to look something up," and snatch the "P" volume of the encyclopedia from under him.

(If you had a question about Salamis, or Sorrento, or the Sistine Chapel, our encyclopedia was no help. Paris had inherited the 1924 edition from London when the London bureau on Bouverie Street got a later edition, but it having been determined that it would be marginally cheaper to mail the encyclopedia to Paris one volume at a time than all at once, that course had been adopted. Unfortunately the "S" volume had not survived the vagaries of the postwar French postal system.)

An excellent newspaperman, Ken Miller had developed some good sources in his couple of years in Paris. One was poor M. Dumaine, the Paris correspondent of, I believe, the *Dépêche du Midi*. In the early and mid fifties the Quai d'Orsay, the French foreign office, was awash with major stories and a key news source. There was the long-standing Indochina war as well as great unrest in French North Africa, particularly in Morocco and Tunisia. And ongoing, delicate negotiations to bring West Germany fully into the Atlantic Alliance without triggering a Soviet response that would endanger the freedom of Berlin.

The Quai d'Orsay gave the international press a daily briefing but kept the hard news for an exclusive higher-level briefing of a carefully selected handful of French diplomatic and regional reporters whose papers supported the government. M. Dumaine was one of these, and he had been suborned by Ken—for a consideration. Every weekday, at around noon, M. Dumaine would walk through the door as unobtrusively as possible. He was a rather pathetic figure, always discreetly turned out in a well-worn very dark suit. His shirt was less than crisp and the tie dark and stringy. He wore a black fedora which he doffed as he entered. He was probably in his sixties, and life had clearly passed him by. He aimed to please. UP's stipend was important to him, his ingratiating manner told us.

His arrival was the signal for Ken to move to a quieter desk at the far end of the room out of earshot. Ken protected his sources from the world, and that included his colleagues. Then, as M. Dumaine took his seat, Ken would get out his lunch. It consisted of a hearty ham and cheese sandwich on a baguette, a thermos of coffee, and a piece of fruit, all carried in an increasingly greasy brown paper bag. Paper bags were rare in Paris at the time, and Ken treated his like an heirloom, folding it up carefully after it had been emptied and stowing it back in his briefcase. Then, as M. Dumaine talked, Ken alternately scribbled notes and chomped away at his sandwich. It was not a pretty sight.

Vanishing News Sources

One of Ken's most valuable contacts was a captain in the Ministry of War who would slip out from time to time to call in some important new development in the Indochina war. UP had no full-time correspondent in Vietnam. We operated with two stringers, one called Louis Gilbert who became less than useful after getting a distinctly unsubtle death threat from the Vietminh in the form of a letter picturing a coffin with the name "Louis Gilbert" on it. The second stringer, Jean Barré was his name, as I recall, turned out after the end of the French-Indochina war to have been in the pay of the Communists all the time he was cabling stories to us. (In UP's view, Mr. Barré was less a villain than the stringer in Algeria who defected to AP the day the revolution erupted.)

We all developed contacts in time, and their phone numbers more often than not were jotted on the inside walls of the telephone booth that stood at the far wall opposite the front door. It was to this booth that we would retreat to take stories dictated in. If you closed the door, which made it unbearably hot in summer, you could shut out newsroom clamor. The booth was equipped with headphones, an aged Smith-Corona portable typewriter, and a desk chair.

Loud were the lamentations one Monday when one of us discovered that in a cleaning jamboree that preceded a visit to the Paris bureau by Roy Howard, boss of Scripps-Howard, our parent company, the walls of the telephone booth had been scrubbed clean, wiping out at one blow a harvest of hard-to-find confidential news sources. It would take months to reconstitute them.

Le Bourgeois Gentilhomme Won't Do

My French was pretty good but I soon found that the vocabulary of *Le Bourgeois Gentilhomme*, which was the kind of thing you studied in French courses, was not adequate to report on a shipwreck off the Brittany coast, an earthquake in Oran, an electric foils tournament, or even a rugby match. The first or second evening that I was alone on the desk on a six to midnight shift, I got a frenetic and totally unheralded call from a stringer. He engulfed me in a torrent of words, not one of which I understood. When I finally got him to pause long enough to find out what this was all about, he told me that he had the results of a very important international rugby match between a Brazilian and a Swedish team.

Well, that at least was a start. I knew there was a game called rugby. I had read *Tom Brown's School Days*, after all, but that was the extent of my knowledge. That *inter droite* was the right wing, I did not at that point know, and it would have been of no help if I had since I didn't know what right wings did on the field. Was it a field? Yes, it must have been a field. The names of the players came across the line as an indigestible goulash of Portuguese sibilants and Swedish consonants. It was hopeless. The man would not slow down.

The teletype operator sitting next to the slot that evening

was vastly amused. Finally he interjected and offered to help take down the story. I handed him the receiver. In no time at all he had written down the scores, the scorers and assists, the nitty-gritty. I sent out the final score and then wrote a short piece—with his assistance.

Remedial steps were obviously in order. The first thing I did was to have a heart-to-heart with Bob Ahier, who agreed to make sure that on those nights that I covered the desk alone I would have (a) a list of all the games scheduled for that evening, and (b) a roster of the players on both teams on hand. (Bob also gave me a fast course on what rugby and soccer are all about, and later on a postgraduate cram session devoted to the Tour de France, which lasts an interminable forty days.)

There's a Word for It

I was one up on most of the American staff in Paris because I had grown up with French. Father had hired Mademoiselle Jeanne Bouchex to be our French governess when Aloïse was five and I two. Mademoiselle was a warm, intelligent woman, and supremely conscientious. She never spoke a word of English to any of us children from the day she walked in the front door to the day she died of cancer a quarter of a century later. Carol, the youngest of our ten, was still only nine. Mademoiselle addressed us always with the formal "vous" rather than the familiar "tu" to ensure that when we in turn addressed adults we would use the proper form. We loved her dearly.

Then, when I was seven, Father, an international oil man, moved the entire family to France for three years. Aloïse and I attended the Cour Fénélon for two years, where we talked and studied in French and all our friends and classmates were French. We were enveloped in the language. We sang *Au Claire de la Lune, Sur le Pont D'Avignon, Savez-vous planter les choux*, and *Frère Jacques* with our friends. We read the Fables of LaFontaine, Perrault's fairy tales, and *The Song of Roland*. We were crushed by Roland and Oliver's deaths at Roncesvalles. Why, oh why, wouldn't Roland blow his horn and bring Charlemagne's mighty army back to fall on the murderous Saracens?

The geography we studied concentrated on France and its widespread empire of colonies and protectorates in North and Equatorial Africa, the Near East, India, and Indochina. I remember being outraged to read in one geography text that Africa was populated by black people, Asia by yellow people, Europe by white people, and America by red people. This was not so, I protested to my classmates. Why, I had never, in my entire life (I was eight at the time) met or seen a single *peau rouge* (redskin). But I'm not sure they believed me.

The history we studied was French history. Charlemagne, William the Bastard who conquered England, St. Louis who went on a crusade and brought home the sacred relics that he housed in the graceful Sainte Chapelle. We wept over Joan of Arc's cruel death, recognized Francis I by his hawk nose and merry eyes, admired Henry of Navarre despite, or maybe because of, his licentiousness. We grieved for *le pauvre petit dauphin* in his cell in the Temple prison, hated Marat and Robespierre, but liked Danton. We spent a great deal of time studying Napoleons I and III. And in that glorious summer in 1933 when Father rented a manor house near Chantilly and we visited the Château de Chantilly, we were able to tell our younger siblings just who Louis Philippe, who had lived there for a while, was. What we hadn't known until those trips to the Château was that the corpulent and unexciting Citizen King had so many handsome soldier sons.

It was during that summer that we first learned to play golf and tennis with our friends, the Cronin twins—Christine and Francine—at the golf and tennis clubs in Chantilly.

So when I arrived in Paris to work at UP I had many advantages. My accent was good and my grasp of French and of French history secure. Irregular verbs and subjunctives tripped off my lips as easily as the scales I was meant to practice every day. It was not until I took a couple of French classes in high school that I perceived that irregular verbs and the subjunctive presented formidable obstacles for people who had not spoken French from birth. But this still wasn't good enough. What I arrived in Paris with in 1953 was, basically, a child's vocabulary.

I needed to broaden that base and broaden it in a hurry. I found it difficult, for instance, when an excited stringer called in to report a train or a shipwreck, to ask the pertinent questions needed to clarify the story. I remember a ferry collision off Calais early on, and trying to get the picture accurately when I didn't know the words for life jacket, lifeboat, or life raft, for tender, trawler, fireboat, or tug, for lighthouse or channel marker. I needed a grownup vocabulary, and I got it through reading French books, going to French movies, listening to the French radio, eavesdropping on French conversations in restaurants, buses, and cafés. In this voyage of discovery I was greatly helped by George Sibera, Bob Rigby, and Nick King, who were as intrigued as I by the niceties of the French language. We couldn't wait to discuss a locution we had come across in conversation, seen in a book or magazine, or overheard.

In only one subject was I head-and-shoulders ahead of my male colleagues, and that was in discussions of the innards of cars. I could identify any part of a car thanks to conferences with every other garage mechanic within a two-hundred kilometer radius of Paris about the perversities of my besotted Hillman-Minx, about which more anon. The word for battery, I would tell them, was *pile*; for gear shift, *boîte de vitesse*; for reverse, *marche arrière*; for bumper, *pare-choc*; for windshield, *pare-brise*; for headlight, *phare*; for clutch, *embrayage*; for brakes, *freins*; for tire, *pneu*; for punctured tire, *pneu crevé*; for multiple punctured tires, *pneus crevés*.

We got a great deal of fun out of literal translations from English to French and French to English. The kind of thing that was later made famous in the book *French Without Tears*. For instance, "She had 'ideas above her station' " would be translated into "*des idées au dessus de sa gare.*" Art Buchwald's column explaining America's celebration of Thanksgiving to the French was a gem of the genre and still appears at *dinde* time in an occasional newspaper fifty years after it was first written. Buchwald was a fixture in the Paris *Herald-Tribune* in the mid-fifties. It was there that he made his reputation. Peter Mayle uses the technique effectively in his popular books about Provence.

My favorite story of the genre was about a friend of my mother's from New Orleans, who had been sent to Paris to study French at the Sorbonne shortly after the Great War. At that time many Parisian bus stops carried a pad with numbered pages nailed to the pole that marked the bus's routes. Passengers would tear off the top number when they arrived and at rush hour the conductor would permit only those with the lower numbers to board. Mother's friend did not understand the procedure. So even though she was first in line on this particular day, conductor after conductor waved her aside in favor of people behind her. Finally, in desperation, she ran down the street after a departing bus, exclaiming piteously: *"Mais, monsieur, je suis gauche dérrière!"*

VLT's War

VLT (pronounced "velthe"), as we called him from the initials at the foot of every take he punched out, was an open-faced young man in his mid or late twenties and a crackerjack teletype operator. He was curious about America, and we talked quite a lot on the quiet Sunday-night shift, which we both frequently worked. Hard pressed for farm hands toward the end of the war, German authorities rounded up teenage French boys to work on German farms. VLT worked for a German farmer but was required at night to return to a prison camp.

Conditions in Germany became chaotic as the Allies advanced toward the Elbe. On the final day of VLT's captivity, a squad of SS men had taken over the camp and marched the twenty or thirty remaining prisoners—all farm laborers—out and into a train tunnel. The SS captain had been ordered to blow up the tunnel and he proposed to do so with the prisoners inside, thus neatly getting them off his hands.

VLT and his friends watched the SS place the dynamite charges. At this point a retreating German Wehrmacht unit arrived on the scene. The major in charge asked the SS captain what was going on and was told.

"But you can't just murder these men," said the major. "Let them go." The SS captain refused. The argument got hot and, VLT told me, the upshot was that the army unit and the SS shot it out. The SS men were routed. The major told the prisoners to head west, that they would very soon run into one of the advance American units and would be taken care of. So VLT got back to his family safe and whole, thanks, as he said with a smile, to one good Boche.

Avenue Wagram

I stayed at the France et Choiseul just a couple of weeks. Yankevitch, one of the front office guys, was anxious to get out of a six-month lease in digs he considered infra dig, and he persuaded me to take the lease off his hands. The situation was far from ideal, but I was anxious to move into a place of my own. What he had to offer was part of an apartment: he rented a large bedroom and bath, a living room, and use of the kitchen from a youngish widow with a five-year-old son, Bruno. She and the boy lived in the back bedroom, which had an adjoining toilet, basin, and shower, and in a small study she had converted into a cramped living room. Madeleine Brancard's husband had died the fall before, suddenly, of cancer. She was making do by writing an astrological column that was syndicated in a number of newspapers and working on the side as a public relations aide for Nina Ricci, handling a lot of their British and American clients. Her English was excellent.

We'd have a cup of coffee or a glass of wine together.

The kitchen, I remember, was filthy but the rooms relatively light and large, and the location was good, on the Avenue Wagram near the Place des Ternes off the Champs Elysée. Once in a while Madeleine and I would have a cup of coffee or a glass of wine together. The arrangement was on the casual side. I admired her bounce and cheerfulness, and for me to have a five-year-old around was fun. Bruno captivated my brother John, who came to visit one afternoon, and he captivated Bruno in turn with a gift of a huge red fire truck that became Bruno's favorite toy.

In the spring with the city emerging from its grey and rainy wintry shroud, Madeleine invited me to spend a weekend in Normandy on the farm her mother still operated with the help of her grandfather. I finagled a Saturday off and motored to Normandy Friday afternoon after my 7 A.M. to 3 P.M. shift. I would return to Paris Sunday in time to work the 6 to midnight shift.

Normandy Weekend

It was a dream farm, situated not far from Yvetot. A large whitewashed farmhouse with thatched roof, several barns and outhouses, and a two-story dovecote that had been done over for Madeleine's doctor sister who spent most of her weekends in Normandy. That's where I was to stay. I reached my quarters on the second floor by climbing up a ladder outside the dovecote to a small platform onto which a door opened. One side of the bed-sitting room had been walled off to accommodate a miniature bathroom. It was whitewashed inside and out. There were, of course, the dozens of small holes in the walls through which the pigeons had flown in and out in the old days. Now they were glassed in. My suitcase was attached to a rope and pulley and hoisted up to me. The bedspread and the easy chair were covered in a yellow and green floral design, the bedside table and lamp and the chair at the small desk were white wicker. It was charming.

Madeleine's mother was as attractive as her daughter, and the grandfather was a winner, a tall man with a bushy white beard, slightly bent now and walking with a cane. Grandpère wore the blue tunic and pants of the Norman farmer and still did a great deal of the work around the farm, which included a dairy herd and several apple orchards. Madeleine had told me that he smoked and I had brought him a carton of Camels from the American businessman's commissary I had recently joined. He was delighted, and embarrassed me by the exuberance of his thanks. Sunday afternoon, after a splendid four-course noonday dinner, I bid them adieu and got back into my unpredictable Hillman Minx for the three-hour-plus drive back to Paris. Grandpère carried my suitcase out and handed me into the car. He had gone into the cellar and brought up a prized bottle of Calvados made from his own apples, which he pressed on me along with a word of wisdom: *"Mademoiselle,"* he warned, *"méfiez-vous des Soixante-quinze."* "Watch out for the 75s," 75 being the last two digits on all Paris license plates, and Paris drivers being well known in the provinces to be wild men. Then he patted me on the shoulder and urged me to come back soon. I would be most welcome, he said, with a wink, "with or without a carton of Camels."

Taxi Drivers Live Here

My next apartment was near the Place d'Italie where, as any Parisian would tell you, the taxi drivers live. Whether all Parisian taxi drivers were domiciled near the Place d'Italie I do not know, but that was what Parisians to a man believed.

A brother and sister who had sat at my table on the SS *Paris* en route to France the summer before, and who were now returning to the States, told me about the apartment they were vacating at 7 Rue Coypel. It was owned by a Catalan anarchist who had fled Spain in the late thirties. She had ended up marrying a Parisian jeweler and they had a little shop on the Rue Monge. Despite her relative affluence, Mme. Hébert, who spoke heavily accented French, remained an unreconstructed anarchist in talk while living a totally bourgeois life. The apartment, a three-floor walk-up, was large and airy and comfortable: two bedrooms, a bathroom with a gas gizmo to heat water for the tub, a sizable entrance hall, large living room, dining room, and kitchen. It was inexpensive since, as all my French friends would kindly explain, it is well known that taxi drivers cannot pay large rents. (Only American journalists in Paris knew that neither could UP correspondents.) It was in a most unfashionable district, which bothered me not at all, although it was at some remove from *le Tout-Paris*. What did bother me was that it was comfortably furnished in the most appallingly bad taste it has ever been my misfortune to live with. Linoleum of squiggly Technicolor design on most of the floors; statuary of large Nubian maidens bearing shelves and lamps and floral garlands; black mahogany tables, polished to a high gloss. Large paintings of scenes of the Catalan equivalent of the dying Indian warrior overlooking a promontory at sunset, pining for his squaw.

Mme. Hébert showed me around herself, telling me where each of the treasures had been bought, and for how much, eliciting exclamations of hollow enthusiasm that put a strain on the adulatory phrases of my as yet limited French vocabulary.

Dear Nick King carried my humongous suitcases up the three flights on his back and collapsed in helpless mirth as I pointed out the treasures that would be all mine for a mere sixty-five dollars a month. I revived him with a dollop of my best Sancerre, which was cooled not on the windowsill, as in my last apartment, but in the large electric refrigerator in the kitchen. Refrigerators were rarities in the kind of apartments we at UP could afford. But nothing was too good for Mme. Hébert's *locataires* (tenants). She found me a cleaning woman, cluck-clucked sadly at the state of what jewelry I had brought, and spirited it away to be cleaned and checked by her husband. Gratis. No, she wouldn't think of taking a penny for it.

Her husband had nothing better to do. She was a sweetie pie underneath all the rough talk.

I Go Genteel

I probably would have spent my entire stay right there with the taxi drivers by the Place d'Italie had not my good friend Wilhelmina (Mina) Wheeler, who worked for the U.S. Embassy, offered me her apartment amid the swells in the sixteenth arrondissement when she received a State Department housing allowance that permitted her to upgrade her own living situation.

M. and Mme. Véron were different kinds of landlords. With Madeleine I had never even talked about a lease; Mme. Hébert was anarchistic in her approach to rents. I simply paid her what my friends had paid her, dropping in with the cash at her little shop sometime within the first week of the month. Mme. Hébert didn't like to discuss money. But M. Véron was an *avocat* of a certain age and everything about the lease of his apartment was spelled out (highly inaccurately as it turned out) in detail. I was invited to tea with Mina. The Vérons' apartment covered the entire second floor of a six-story apartment house at 6 Rue Eugène Delacroix, just off the Rue de la Pompe and the Avenue Henri Martin, near the old Trocadéro. This was the neighborhood we had lived in when I was a child in Paris in the early thirties. One Avenue Ingres, where we had had a tall angular house with stained-glass windows, was just one metro stop further down the line; and still later we had lived in a huge apartment at 26 Avenue Henri Martin. It was familiar territory, and I felt at once at home here. It was also rather closer to the action than the dear old thirteenth arrondissement's Place d'Italie.

The Vérons, who were retired—they must have been in their early seventies—occupied the front section of the original apartment. My apartment was carved out of what must at one time have been the kitchen and maid's quarters: it had long halls with lots of closet space, a reasonable kitchen, nice living room, and small bedroom with a connecting bath. It was simple and rather dark, looking out as it did on a smallish court with an outsized chestnut tree that provided shade winter and summer.

After tea, at which little mention had been made of the reason for it, Mina reported that the Vérons had found me very *convenable*. They would be delighted to rent me their apartment upon the recommendations of the charming Mlle Wheeler de l'ambassade des Etats-Unis. Mina brought me an inventory of the furnishings of the apartment which I was to sign and return to M. Véron. The only problem was that it had very little to do with what furnishings were actually there. It didn't matter, said Mina. This was probably the inventory they drew up thirty years ago when their youngest child moved out. It was just a formality, she assured me. She had signed it and so had her predecessor. So I signed, reluctantly. Mina was right. The inventory was never mentioned again.

Mina acted as middleman in these negotiations. The rent would be payable every three months, in advance. It would be payable in the French franc equivalent of $252 ($84 a month) in French bills, not by check. M. Veron would put a note under my door when the rent became due inviting me to tea some afternoon the following week. I would arrive. We would have a pleasant tea, with small *pâtisseries* and a great deal of small talk. At the conclusion of the tea, Mme. Véron would excuse herself. M. Véron would move from the easy chair to his desk, indicating the shift from social to business mode. He would tick off my phone calls: we shared a line for reasons I never really understood but which were very important to M. Véron. He would add in the rent of the gas refrigerator Mina had had installed in the kitchen. (The refrigerator people insisted on billing the owner of the apartment, the Vérons, not the locataire, Mina or me.) M. Véron would add these two items to the 88,200 francs I owed for the rent, and I would peel off the appropriate number of thousand- and hundred-franc notes.

The Milkman of Avenue Ingres

Setting up housekeeping in Paris was, well, different. My most agreeable and helpful concierge found me a cleaning woman, the concierge of the apartment building across the street, who came in for two or three hours once a week and did my personal laundry. But the sheets and towels, on Mina's advice, I rented, carrying a set to the laundry once a week and retrieving the second.

I did most of my shopping at the greengrocer's around the corner to the right on Rue de la Tour, but for milk, cream, butter, cheese, and eggs I went to the *laiterie*, for bread and the morning croissant to the *boulangerie*, for meat to the *boucherie*, for wine and aperitifs to Nicolas, and for delicacies to a tiny *épicerie* that offered, among other expensive delectables, vegetables fresh-cooked late every afternoon for the benefit of working women. I was exceedingly fond of their creamed spinach, sliced carrots, *petits pois*, and artichokes. I took to keeping a *filet*, the string bag that seemed an appendage of every French housewife, in my car. These little neighborhood stores did not provide their customers with paper bags at this time, but they would, grumpily, wrap your purchases in an old newspaper if absolutely necessary. All of these establishments were within two blocks of my apartment and over the months I came to have a better than nodding acquaintance with their owners and staffs.

I dropped in at the local cleaners to pick up clothes one afternoon and asked for them in the name of Buckley (*Bu-que-let*). The woman behind the counter wanted to know if, *par hasard*, I knew of a Reid Buckley, or perhaps a Jimmy Buckley? They were my brothers, I told her. She, it turned out, had worked for Mother for three or four weeks in the winter of 1932 when six or seven of the young Buquelets had come down with measles, followed in short order by chicken pox, and Mother had hired an extra hand to help nurse the children and carry the trays up and down the narrow steps of the house at 1 Avenue Ingres. She remembered Reid fondly, so sunny and bright, but Zimmie (the future United States senator, undersecretary of state, and federal judge), was, back then when she knew him, *un peu méchant*. In a word, mischievous.

As I started to leave, she asked about my father. Was he well? Alas, he was not well, I told her. He had suffered a couple of strokes and was partially paralyzed. It astonished me that she asked about Father rather than Mother, with whom she had dealt on a daily basis. She told me that Father had been considered *un homme formidable* in the *quartier*. He had arrived out of the blue, and set up house with his wife and seven (soon

He had bought a Jersey cow
and brought her back to Paris.

to be nine) children, a French governess (this they understood), but also two Mexican nurses and a Negro *homme de ménage*, dear James Cole, in the fall of 1929 when the whole world was falling to pieces. This, in itself, was sufficiently bizarre. But when Father had discovered that he could not buy pasteurized milk in the local laiterie, or in any laiterie within easy distance of 1 Avenue Ingres, this in the land of Louis Pasteur, what had he done? This question was accompanied by a supremely Gallic shrug of the shoulders. Why, he had boarded a Channel ferry for the Isle of Jersey, bought a Jersey cow, and brought her back to Paris. What made him truly formidable in the estimation of the quartier was that he had then managed to persuade the caretaker of a large establishment down the street—usually a difficult man—to take care of the cow, milk her twice a day, and twice a day cross the avenue with a foaming pail of creamy Jersey milk for the denizens of 1 Avenue Ingres! An impressive performance. She was, she told me, sorry, truly sorry, to hear of Father's physical problems and hoped I would remember her to him when next I wrote. Although, *bien sûr*, he would not remember her.

A Nostalgic Note

It is a little later that fall. The apartment has shaped up nicely, and now looks pleasantly lived in. There are books in the bookcases, pictures on the walls, family photographs here and there, two new floor lamps, ashtrays around, and a small radio perched on the desk, tuned to one of a number of classical music stations. I am sitting comfortably in my easy chair. The bulb in the table lamp is bright enough to read by with ease. Although there's a nip in the air—it's early October—I am warm and cozy. The gurgling in the radiator pipes is music to my ears, promising as it does, warmth to my tootsies.

The phone rings. It's George Bibikoff.

"George, what are you doing in Paris? I thought you were building electric grids in Camaroon?"

George laughs, and says he is home for three or four days to consult with the head office. His mother has told him that I am now living in Paris, and could I possibly be free for supper?

Suddenly I am back five years in a very different Paris. In 1948 not only Paris but all of France was still in a state of moral and physical disarray following the devastations of World War II. I had quit UP in New York right after the GOP convention that nominated Thomas E. Dewey for president that summer, and taken off for Paris with my sister Patricia for a couple of months. Father had written his very good friend, Count Valerian Nicolievich Bibikoff ("Bibi"), that we were coming, and before we knew it we had become protégées of Bibi and his wife, and friends of their son George, who was our age and finishing up his studies as an electrical engineer.

The Paris of 1948 was drab, dark, dirty, cold, and generally demoralized, a far less inviting Paris than the one I am currently finding so entrancing. Everything back then was still in short supply, or rationed: bread, meat, sugar, coffee, gasoline. Many necessities that were not rationed were impossible to find, like, say, heat.

Trish and I had run out of money so we were quartered for the last two weeks of our stay in the cold and drafty apartment of a White Russian émigré, Princess Irina Kurakina, to whom Bibi had introduced us. The arrangements were that Patricia and I would rent the apartment but that Irina would retain use of her bedroom. In practice all the facilities, meager as they were, were used by all. Irina was much too much fun to segregate in a tiny back bedroom.

Irina was one of the lucky White Russians just then. Most of them were suspected by French authorities of having collaborated with the Germans to overthrow the hated Soviets and a great number of them had indeed done just that, including dear Bibi. After the invasion of Russia he had signed on as an interpreter with the German army and had come to within ten miles of his ancestral home before the tide turned at Leningrad. For this conduct French authorities had confiscated his phone. "They took from me my telephone, those idiots," he complained. They could have imprisoned him or expelled him, but with no proof that the Nazis had *not* drafted him, they settled on depriving him of the convenience of a phone. Bibi's wife Sophy—who was Leo Tolstoy's niece, the Countess Tolstoy—had wisely burned the letters Bibi had sent her from Russia while working with the Nazis.

Irina had landed a plum of a job as secretary to the local boss of the Marshall Plan who operated from the U.S. Embassy. She was a terrible secretary, she told us. Her shorthand was almost nonexistent, she was a poor typist, and on top of that terribly disorganized personally, as we who lived in her apartment could attest. But she spoke two or three languages exceedingly well and could get along in another couple. That wasn't what assured her job, however. Her boss wouldn't think of firing her, she told us, because he got such a kick out of saying, "My secretary, Princess Kurakina, will take care of it." Or, "I'll ask Princess Kurakina to look it up in the files." It was heaven for a young man from Kansas to have a secretary who was a bona fide princess.

But the bona fide princess, like the Little Princess in the attic, had no heat. In the Paris of 1948 landlords were not required to turn on the heat in their frequently porous apartment buildings until December 1, and didn't. The only heat in Irina's apartment was provided by a portable electric radiator which we pulled and shoved from room to room.

Election Day was approaching, and Patricia and I assured our White Russian friends that Tom Dewey would be elected. They scoffed at us. They wanted Truman elected because Truman had initiated the Marshall Plan, which was giving France what hope it had of recovery. They were rabidly anti-Communist, but they didn't blame Truman for the loss of Czechoslovakia to the Communists in the summer of 1948 because it had been Roosevelt, not Truman, who had given way to Stalin's demands at Yalta and sealed the fate of Eastern Europe for nearly half a century. What's more, Truman had stood up to the Communists in Greece and Turkey. Ergo, Truman not only deserved to, but would be elected.

From your viewpoint, we told Bibi and his friends, Truman may be a good president, but the American people are tired of the Democratic Party after sixteen years in power. You really don't know what you are talking about. You can take it from us, Dewey will be the next president of the United States of America! We were insufferably pompous.

We turned on the radio the morning after Election Day, and were, as Bibi would have put it, "consternated." We didn't bother to get dressed. We were warmer in our flannel pajamas, woolen bathrobes, overcoats, gloves, and wool socks. We could only use the radiator sparingly because there wasn't enough power to run it and the radio at the same time. Within a minute of plugging them both in, the fuse would blow. (In those days in Paris, you didn't replace a worn fuse with a new one. You removed the defective unit and laboriously wound a silver cord made of something or other important, around it, and put it back in the fuse box, a time-consuming enterprise.) So mostly we listened to the extraordinary, the unbelievable electoral news coming in over the radio.

At noon the door burst open and in strode a triumphant Bibi. "Prichilla, Patrushka, up, up! We must go celebrate Truman's brilliant victory. In politics," this last with huge condescension, "you are as babies—as babies!" So, it was up, up! and soon we were on our way to yet another dark little grocery store whose proprietor, not infrequently a former White Russian general, at the sight of Valerian Bibikoff, would leap into the back room and pour four little cups of vodka for dear Valerian and his friends and of course himself, to be followed in short order by four more and a zakuska or two.

It was indeed a different Paris back then in 1948. To drive into the country you'd have to procure gas coupons by one means or another, and be sure you had a fifth tire in the boot because you would certainly need it. There were few tourists in

Europe as yet, and accommodations were hard to find, and often rough (no running water). Paris itself was drab. Most of the fountains had been turned off to conserve energy, and by night the streets were dimly illuminated.

But by 1953 all that had changed. Now, on holidays and the occasional summer weekend, the great monuments of the central city are ablaze with light: the Arc de Triomphe, the Eiffel Tower, Notre Dame, the Place Vendôme, the Place de la Concorde, the Madeleine, the Palais Bourbon, Sacré Coeur. Today, in 1953, I realized France had turned an important corner on its comeback trail. Water now cascades in the fountains at the Concorde, newly planted flower beds brighten the Tuileries and Luxembourg gardens. Still ahead, some years ahead, are Charles de Gaulle and André Malraux's extravagant vision of Paris with its face scrubbed free of the grime of centuries.

I hadn't realized until I remembered that oddball Election Day in 1948 what a difference the intervening five years had made.

Done in by Hillman Minx

Doing business in France was filled with surprises, many of which came down to the fact that the French wanted as few transactions as possible to appear on their books where the *fisc* (the French internal revenue) could go after them. Everything was done on a cash basis, no need even to open a checking account.

I wanted a car, preferably a cheap but serviceable convertible. Once again Mina came to the rescue, producing an embassy friend who had just been transferred back to Washington and wanted to get rid of his beige Hillman Minx, with its smashing crimson leather upholstery, in haste. It was only three years old, and he could let me have it for $500. It had a great advantage in that it already had red TT plates, so these would not have to be renegotiated with the authorities. TT stood for Temporary Transit, and it meant that any foreigner (or at least any American) could buy a car in France without paying the stiff internal tax, providing said foreigner agreed to take it out of the country or dispose of it otherwise within two years of purchase. This had been enacted for the benefit of the hordes of Americans detached for a stint, frequently of only a few weeks or months, in France in the Marshall Plan years. They needed cars, but were reluctant to pay two-thirds again what they would have had to pay for them in the States.

I got the initial paperwork done for the transfer of owner-ship in the international AAA office off the Champs Elysée, and was then instructed to go to the French motor vehicle department to get new TT plates. This proved more compli-cated than you would have thought. The man behind the desk reaffirmed that the paperwork was in order and handed me a slip of paper on which was written "TT 643875": my registra-tion number. This I was instructed to take to any local garage and there have my plates made. There were some restrictions. They had to be red, with white lettering, but they could be rectangular, or square, or round or really any shape I desired providing it could be attached to the front and rear bumpers of the most miserable car I have ever owned.

The principal problem with my particular Hillman Minx was a condition called *"le démarreur coincé."* The *démarreur* is the starter. When you turned the key in the ignition, as I was given to understand, a wheel with spikes on it rotated, and when it engaged, a spike fitting into a designated crevice, the engine turned over. All well and good, but *hélas,* on my wheel, one spike was missing, had been mislaid somewhere down the line. And when, Russian roulette–wise, the wheel stopped turning at that perilous point, nothing happened. Worse than nothing happened. The car froze solid, like a clipper ship in the Arctic ice. The wheel wouldn't turn, the wipers wouldn't go, the lights if on, stayed on, if off, stayed off. The whole thing was in the vehicular equivalent of rigor mortis, and the only way to get it started was to get out, raise the hood, prop it up, reach into its innards with a gloved hand holding a pair of pliers, and turn the démarreur a half inch or so. Then close the hood, remove the glove, slip into the driver's seat, turn the key in the ignition, hold your breath and implore *le bon Dieu* to let a spike hit the jackpot this time round.

The difficulties of this procedure in the customary evening traffic jam at the Place de l'Alma with a bus on your tail, driver's hand on horn, motorists screaming at you, and the gendarme headed in your direction, were frightful and frightening. And it was hard to explain to an agitated Parisian chauffeur. Best, as I soon discovered—for this happened to me numerous times—was to pocket the key at the instant the steering wheel froze heralding a démarreur coincé, slide swiftly across to the passenger side, slip out that door, and head for the metro. By the time the frustrated motorists had worked themselves into a frenzy at the small sleek beige coupe with its flame-red leather seats impeding forward movement, I would be safely en route to the Rue de la Pompe, by metro, and thence the block or two to Eugène Delacroix.

At the garage next to 6 Rue Eugène Delacroix, Ahmed, the Moroccan evening attendant, would roar with laughter as he watched me approach on foot. *"Alors, vous êtes encore en panne,"* (you've broken down again) he would exclaim, *"mais c'est impossible,"* and laugh again. Yes, I would admit. I am en panne. "Not the Place de l'Alma?" Yes, yes, at the Place de l'Alma, *comme d'habitude*, and I would hand Ahmed my key (and a reasonable piece of change). Sometime in the middle of the night, he would take the metro to the Place de l'Alma, lift the hood, apply the pliers, and slink into the driver's seat of the abandoned Hillman, which by this time had usually been pushed to the side, as out of the way as possible in that crowded six-way intersection, and bring it home to its roost.

The *démarreur coincé* was but one of the many maladies that afflicted not only my Hillman but every Hillman I knew in Paris. Mina's and Nick King's were like mine in two things: they were snappy-looking, which was why we bought them, and as disaster prone as Abbott and Costello. When any of us would plan an excursion the first question asked was: Does your Hillman "march"?—a locution we picked up from the pained expression of our *garagistes* when told that, once again, *"Ça ne marche pas."* The Paris mechanics got no help from the manufacturer back in England. In the nearly three years that my Hillman and I kept company—quite often stationary company—the manufacturer was unable to find a replacement démarreur for my faulty model or to locate and send to Paris two yellow headlights that French law required me to use at night. My helpful garagiste finally painted my headlights yellow.

Our Man at le Palais de Justice

M. Beaupré was our man at the Palais de Justice. He was paid to alert us to any story that might be used on the international wire. And there weren't many of these. But to make sure he got his monthly retainer M. Beaupré called in on a regular basis. When local stringers called Mlle. Henri, the telephone operator, she would look around the room, see who was not busy or obviously malingering, and call out. She used the men's last names: King, Rigby, Miller, but addressed me always as Mlle. Buckley (*Buquelet*).

Mlle. Henri was not to be trifled with. She was a tall woman, five eight or so, and imposing, not fat but solid. She had one of those incredibly long, heavy French noses that French women seem to be able to carry off. Mlle. Henri's was always covered with a thin dusting of powder considerably lighter than her complexion. (Could it have been the rice powder we read about in Victorian novels?) She wore her hair in a severe bun and dressed in simple light-colored print dresses in summer and darker colored print dresses in winter, often, summer and winter, covered by a beige or brown or black cardigan. She was very sensitive, sitting as she did by the front door, to *les courants d'air* and amused us no end by complaining—loudly—when one of us left the door on the telephone cabinet open. She said that it created a courant d'air, and gave her *frissons*, and would King, or Rigby, or Mlle. Buckley, or Miller, please keep it shut, as she had asked us so *many* times.

As the newest member of the staff and consequently the least busy, I got M. Beaupré quite often in those first few weeks when I was finding my way around. Finally he became my man at le

Palais de Justice. When he called in, Mlle. Henri would look my way and, with the loosening of the regulation tightness of her lips which passed for a smile, announce: "M. Beaupré, for his *chère amie*." Followed by what can only be described as a smirk.

Since few of the stories M. Beaupré had to report were urgent, M. Beaupré got into the habit of chatting about this and that. He told me some stories that tickled his fancy in a high, almost feminine pitch of voice that accorded so strangely with his bulky six four frame.

Gallic Tall Tales

It was he who recounted to me in rollicking detail the unfolding story of a bunch of Corsican criminals who had, in effect, taken over the ancient prison of Pont l'Evêque in Normandy.

They had bribed the new warden, an easygoing fellow, and in no time at all they had reorganized Pont l'Evêque to suit their needs, from breakfast in bed served to the "caids," the chiefs, by the less well situated convicts, to cognac with their after-dinner cigars. They spent swanky weekends in hotels in Le Touquet and Deauville, had their girlfriends in for extended visits; in short, lived the Corsican equivalent of the life of Riley. If one of them on a weekend pass failed to return,

From breakfast in bed to cognac with their after-dinner cigar.

they waited until his sentence was up and forged his release documents with an array of stamps and forms they had stolen.

What brought the whole ridiculous operation down was when hardened felons awaiting trial started confessing to crimes, real and imaginary, committed in Normandy in order to be sent to Pont l'Evêque, which under this regime swelled from a complement of twenty prisoners to nearly a hundred. Why was this so? some of the prosecutors asked themselves, and the sorry details soon came to light. M. Beaupré and I had a glorious ride on that story, which UP broke and pretty much controlled for a couple of days. Years later, the story of the happy prisoners of Pont l'Evêque made a brief appearance on Broadway as a musical comedy.

M. Beaupré's most amusing story, the exact details of which are a little vague in my memory, had to do with two retired naval officers living in a shabby apartment building in the second arrondissement. They and their wives played bridge two or three times a week and were good friends. Neither couple had a telephone—at that time, hard to get in Paris—so they took to communicating by pounding out messages on the water pipes that ran along one side of the walls from Commandant Perrier's apartment on the first floor to Commandant Nicaud's on the fifth. Mostly it was: we will be ten minutes late, or meet you at the door, that sort of thing.

But, M. Beaupré said, chère amie, you will not believe this but it is true, I assure it to you. One evening they had a fight over their bridge game, and the Nicauds left in a huff to climb the four flights to their apartment. Nicaud was so mad that he went directly to the pipe and tapped out a message casting doubts on the maternal antecedents of Mme. Perrier. Commandant Perrier hurtled up the stairs, punched Commandant Nicaud in the nose, and demanded that he wipe out the insult on the field of honor, and stomped downstairs again.

There it might have ended, said M. Beaupré, but alas, neither spouse would permit her husband to fight a duel—the old fools might hurt each other—so in frustration, Perrier took Nicaud to court. He charged Nicaud with having libeled Mme. Perrier (not to say her mother). What was at issue was whether any of the tenants in the apartments on the left side of the building on the second, third, and fourth floors understood the Morse code, and, of course, if any of them did, were they listening in that night? Did they hear the libel? For the life of me I can't remember how the case came out. But it was the occasion of my only face-to-face meeting with M. Beaupré, who invited me to celebrate the verdict—whatever it was— and our so charming collaboration, with a *petit coup de vin* at a little bistro he favored near le Palais de Justice.

I Get Religion

Bob Ahier bounces through the door in full cry. "Priscilla," he announces to everyone in the newsroom who will listen, "is as crazy as all these other Americans."

And he proceeds to tell them just why. Robert and I had hurried out for a quick lunch at a small workman's eating place near the Bourse. Graciousness was not the major attraction of this establishment, but the price was right and the food surprisingly good. You sat at long bare wooden trestle tables where for 350 francs (one buck) you were served a three-

course meal with a quarter-liter of barely potable rough Alger-
ian red wine. (The white wine was not potable.) If you wanted
a napkin, a strip of paper torn off a roll of paper toweling, it
was 10 francs extra. For your 350 francs you got a first course of
soup in winter, an hors d'oeuvre of some sort in spring, summer, and fall, an entrée, meat or fish, and a piece of fruit or a
slice of cheese for dessert. Coffee was extra and not worth
whatever it cost.

On this particular day, after we had paid our 350 francs, the
waiter asked, *"Maigre ou gras?"* ("Thin or fat?"), meaning fish
or fowl, or more precisely, this being Lent, were you fasting or
not? *"Gras,"* said Bob, *"Maigre,"* said I. "But Peets," said
Robert, who had glanced around at the other diners, "they're
serving quail today." "I know, Robert," I said, "but this is Lent
and I'm fasting" as all good Catholics were expected to do
prior to Vatican II.

That's what had done it.

"Can you imagine," Bob proceeded to broadcast to the
newsroom, "Priscilla actually fasts," and everyone laughed.
How innocent these Americans were. Only Mlle. Henri, who
I suspected also fasted, failed to join the general hilarity.

This is how I became UP's religious correspondent. When
Billy Graham ("the apostle in gabardine" in the supercilious
French press) came to town, it was I, because I knew all about
religion, who was sent to cover his nightly meetings and to
bring back a count for UP's Southern newspaper clients on just
how many Frenchmen had made "a decision for Christ" that
evening. After the first night's rally I found Billy Graham's PR
man, Paul, and arranged to meet him at the conclusion of
every meeting and get the exact number of decisions for Christ

made that evening, which would obviate having to sit through seven successive evenings of Billy Graham exhortations. But one night, Paul wasn't to be found. Trying to get backstage I became entangled in the line of those "making a decision for Christ." The officials charged with herding the repentant sinners to the small rooms where they would receive further instructions would not let me break away. Finally, in the loudest possible voice, I exclaimed: "But I do *not* want to make a decision for Christ!" Silence in the hall as dozens of about-to-be-reborn Christians shook their heads sadly at a sinner fallen by the wayside. Only 127 cynical and sinful Parisians made a decision for Christ that night, not the 128 they had counted on.

It was in the role as religious reporter that I became M. Abbad's man at 2 Rue des Italiens. M. Abbad was UP's stringer in Lourdes, and had been on the job nearly ten years, ever since the UP Paris bureau reopened in the final months of World War II. He was thoroughly bored with his assignment. The phone would ring. Mlle. Henri would motion me to the telephone booth. "*C'est M. Abbad pour vous, Mlle. Buckley,*" she would announce, and I would move with some reluctance into the booth. M. Abbad had a heavy Provençal accent and sounded dispirited; not only sounded, he was dispirited. We would go through the routine. The pilgrimage that arrived today at 10:32 A.M., only thirty minutes late, was from County Cork. It consisted of three bishops—we would pause while he spelled out their names—four priests, nine nuns, and 238 pilgrims, eighteen of them on stretchers or in wheelchairs. Four days later M. Abbad would call to announce that the pilgrims had departed with eighteen pilgrims still on stretchers or in wheelchairs and another contingent would be arriving two days later. These bone-dry stories made for a long spring and summer pilgrimage season for both M. Abbad and me, and presumably for the pilgrims, as well.

M. Abbad was not a chatterer like dear M. Beaupré at the Palais de Justice, whose calls I always welcomed, but one day when he seemed in less of a hurry to ring off than usual, I asked him whether in the thirty-odd years he had been covering Lourdes for a variety of news organizations he had ever himself witnessed a miracle. He hesitated, then said, yes, just once.

He told me this story. It had been in the mid-forties. One of the pilgrims on a train from Paris who was obviously in extremis was carried off the train on his stretcher, cursing, swearing, and blaspheming. He didn't want to be here, he didn't believe in this religious crap, there was no God, he was an atheist and a Communist and wanted only to be left to die in peace in his own bed. His wife, old and worn, anxious and scandalized, tried to hush him but without success. It was she, worried for the salvation of his eternal soul, who was bringing him to Lourdes against his will now that he was physically too weak to resist. The next morning he attended the pilgrim's Mass, still cursing and swearing, and cursing and swearing was carried into the Grotto and bathed in the waters of Lourdes.

A week later, said M. Abbad, I saw that man walk back and climb aboard the train without help. His color was good, he walked with the vigor of a man much younger, to all intents and purposes it had been a miraculous cure.

"But was he really cured?" I asked. "No, he was not," said M. Abbad.

"Two years later, there he was again, on a stretcher coming off the train. His cancer had reappeared, he had only a week or two to live. I questioned him and he told me that indeed it had been a miracle. 'I'm going to die,' he said, 'but I am going to die in the Church, having received the last rites. The miracle was not that my body was cured, but that I regained my faith.' "

Gloria Swanson and I

Working for United Press entailed more than just chasing down and delivering the news. You did what you were told to do no matter what it was. Which is how I came to meet Gloria Swanson. This was shortly after her sensational comeback in *Sunset Boulevard*. She was all the rage and had recently embarked in the couture business with a line of inexpensive, tasteful women's clothes. Some big dome at Scripps-Howard had signed her up to do a weekly newspaper column hoping to capitalize (spell that MAKE MONEY) off her new popularity. They envisioned a chatty column filled with amusing anecdotes, recollections of Hollywood's golden years, of its glamorous Romeos and vamps. Gloria Swanson envisioned a series of enlightening essays on the philosophy of Gloria Swanson liberally laced with comments and thoughts on diet, exercise, and the healthy life.

The column was not selling. Newspapers wanted what Scripps-Howard wanted, not what Miss Swanson was turning out. So New York messaged Paris, where Gloria Swanson was then living, ordering that Buckley take Swanson to lunch and instruct her on what was wanted in her column ("beat some sense into her head," was the way the message read). This is not the kind of assignment I like. What's more, I was, of course, worried about what I would wear. But most of all I worried that I would end up financially in the hole. Would United Press stand still for the kind of restaurant Miss Swanson was likely to pick?

I called, and she suggested La Crémaillère, which was as I had feared one of Paris's swankiest eateries on the Faubourg St. Honoré, hard by the Elysée Palace, the French White House. I was given a 10,000-franc advance which I feared would buy only an hors d'oeuvre, and headed out.

I was lunching with Miss Swanson, I told the headwaiter, and spotted her at once at a table, chatting with Adolphe Menjou, looking exactly the way he had looked in *Little Miss Marker*, dapper, dapper, dapper. I went up and introduced myself. Menjou jumped to his feet, and as he pulled out my chair and seated me, asked: "Are you any relation of Bill Buckley?" "Why, yes," I replied, much surprised. "He's my brother."

"What a charming, talented young man," Menjou enthused, and turning to Gloria Swanson explained that he had met Bill recently in Hollywood where Bill had been trying to raise money to start a conservative weekly (*National Review*) from Hollywood's conservative community, from men like himself, Ward Bond, Bing Crosby, John Wayne, Morrie Ryskind, and others.

He excused himself and joined his waiting friends a few minutes later, and Gloria started to tell me what she planned to do with her column. She waved the menu a waiter started to put before us airily aside. "I will have a small omelette *fines herbes*," she said. That's all. I hastily ordered the same.

You might say that it was a Gloria Swanson lunch. She took charge of the conversation and listened to not a single one of the editorial suggestions I made. I could just as successfully have been lecturing one of those stone heads on Easter Island. It was a total bust except that the bill came to just under 10,000 francs.

I made one or two more attempts, all equally futile. A few weeks later Scripps-Howard folded the column. But Gloria invited me to her apartment a couple of times thereafter for a cup of tea. I liked her, but at a cautious remove. She dressed with great flair, was at once soignée and outrée, reminding me of my mother in looks if not in manner. She was tough and took no guff from anyone. But as long as you kept at arm's length—and understood that a tea with Gloria was a Gloria tea—it was a bracing experience.

Jane Russell vs. Christian Dior

I did a feature one day on Jane Russell trying to struggle into one of Christian Dior's new H-(*haricots verts*) line creations that ended up getting front page play all over America and brought me to the attention of the editors back in New York. The piece started: "When an irresistible force meets an immovable object something must give. In the case of curvaceous Jane Russell and fashion designer Christian Dior, it turned out to be the seams." The byline, one of my first, was P. L. Buckley (not Priscilla Buckley), since Ed Korry and the Paris bureau were still trying to conceal from Al Bradford, UP's ferocious European manager (whose headquarters were at some remove in Bonn), that, against Mr. Bradford's express orders, a woman had been hired on the Paris news staff.

New York saw the situation differently. Since I was there,

and by now well established, they might as well exploit me. They started assigning me stories for the Red Letter, a weekly UP feature supplement designed for the then ubiquitous newspaper Sunday magazines.

Of Salads, and Kings

One was to do a story on French dressing. In the States at the time if you ordered French dressing it came out of a bottle and was of a glutinous opaque orange color and sweet of taste. It had absolutely no resemblance to anything a Frenchman would put on lettuce. What to do? That year Michelin listed five three-star Paris restaurants in its annual guide. I wrote the chefs of all five and asked for their recipe for salad dressing. The Tour d'Argent and Café de Paris did not reply. That surprised me, particularly from the Tour d'Argent, which was then as now so tourist-oriented, but I did hear from Lapérouse, Maxim's, and Le Grand Véfour. Lapérouse said, briefly, that it used only the finest Italian olive oil in its dressing and it was that that made it so distinctive. Maxim's chef invited me to see his kitchen, and told me that the secret of Maxim's dressing was that the vinegar came from the cellars of, it was either Château Margaux or Haut Brion, and only from the grapes in the finest vintage years.

But my heart was won over by Le Grand Véfour, where I was invited to lunch. The chef made his appearance at about cheese time, bringing a bowl and some ingredients to demonstrate how the dressing was made. Their secret was that in addition to using the finest Italian olive oil, and the very highest grade wine vinegar, they included in their dressing very finely chopped chicken liver. The livers must come from the acknowledged aristocrats of the French poultry world, hens born and raised in the region of Bresse. "This last was the most important," the chef assured me.

One up for Le Grand Véfour.

On another of these Red Letter assignments, this one on what Europe's exiled royalty were up to, the maître d' at Maxim's regaled me with an amusing story. Ex-King Peter of Yugoslavia had reserved a table for two, and he didn't come and didn't come. Late in the evening the Duke and Duchess of Windsor turned up, and after a short wait were given the only vacant table. When Peter finally made his appearance, the headwaiter rushed to him and tried to explain. "After all," said the head waiter, "the Duke of Windsor was the King of England." "But I *am* the King of Yugoslavia," Peter snapped, and turned on his heels and stalked out.

Dmitri's Story

It was George Sibera's day off and he was working at his second job at Radio Free Europe. He sounded disturbed and asked if I could meet him at a little café off the Boulevard St. Germain, in the St. Séverin area. George was evasive about why he wanted to meet me, but he said there was a story in it for UP. UP bigwigs were starchy about letting George file stories he came across in his work for RFE on the UP wire. They resented his moonlighting at RFE even though he wasn't paid enough to support a wife and two children.

As we sat over a cup of coffee, George shied away from explaining why he had called me. "I want you to make up your own mind about it," he said, and, abruptly, "Shall we go? They'll be waiting for us."

We walked into one of those dingy dark, earthy-smelling small hotels that dot the area, past an uncaring desk clerk, and up a flight of stairs dimly lit by the *minuterie*. At the first landing, a stocky fellow looked us over, spoke a few words to George, and motioned us on up. We passed two other guards before we reached the fourth floor where yet a fourth man opened the door for us into a tiny, dark bedroom, sparsely furnished with a large bed, a washbasin, an armoire, one chair, and a small table. On the bed lay a man in heavy wool pajamas. When he turned toward the door I saw that his face was battered, a black eye, cuts on the cheekbones, a bruised mouth. One of the men pulled up the pajama pants to show me deep cuts and bruises up and down his legs. "Boots," said George.

The man on the bed, I'll call him Dmitri, told me his story in such halting French that George finally had him tell it in Romanian. A Romanian then translated it for George in German, who told it to me in French.

This was during the coldest days of the cold war when there was virtually no communication between East and West. Dmitri was a World War II displaced person, a German slave laborer who had drifted west as the war ended and sought refuge in France where he was now living in freedom, if in penury, as an unskilled laborer. He had heard that a Romanian folk dancing troupe would perform in Paris and borrowed enough money to buy a good orchestra seat. As the lights went down he recognized in the orchestra a childhood friend, the first person he had seen from the place of his birth in eight long years. At the intermission Dmitri tried excitedly to talk to the man, but was brushed away. During the second act, however, an usher brought him a note, an appointment to meet his friend at the Gare d'Orsay Hotel, where the Romanian troupe was staying, at three the next afternoon.

Part of the abandoned Gare d'Orsay was at this time a shabby hotel, renovated on the cheap after the war as a temporary measure to help ease the hotel room shortage in Paris. It bore no resemblance to the elegant Musée d'Orsay that today occupies the old railroad station.

Dmitri could hardly wait. He had had no news of his family and friends for so long. At three on the dot, he knocked at the door. His friend embraced him, and as he did so, the door to the connecting room was flung open and four Romanian goons—part of the secret police contingent sent along to keep the folk dancers in line—burst in and started to beat Dmitri. His friend left the room without a backward glance. Dmitri was knocked to the ground. They were kicking him in the legs and ribs when a chambermaid rushed in, took one look, and ran off to return with a policeman. The head goon explained that they had caught Dmitri, a sneak thief, at work, and would take care of his punishment themselves.

Not in France, said the gendarme, politely but firmly, and helped Dmitri up, and out. Once in the street, he told Dmitri that there would be no charge against him, he, the gendarme, knew perfectly well what those *salopards* were up to. He urged Dmitri to report his beating to the police, and when he refused, offered to take him to a clinic. But Dmitri wanted only to get away. He fled to the hotel whose concierge was another Romanian exile, which was where I found him. His hurts were deep, but the deepest, the one he kept going back to, was one to which he would never know the answer: had his old friend betrayed him? had he set him up for a beating? or perhaps even a kidnapping? He thought so. His friends disagreed with the last. Dmitri was of no importance to the regime, they argued, but his beating, that was a "sign" that the refugee community could understand. It would be a long time before another Romanian exile tried to contact a traveling troubadour.

I walked out sick at heart. I filed the story and it went out. I didn't mention that it was George who had put me on to it. Whether it got any play I don't know, that's one of the frustrations of wire service work. You write it, it goes out, and very seldom do you hear any more about it. There was no feedback, no requests for further interviews. Perhaps the public was tired of the Dmitris of this world and their everlasting complaints. A year or so later Hungarian students took to the streets against their puppet leaders and their Soviet overlords, and got little more support from the West than had poor Dmitri.

The Great Pétain Flap

It's a Sunday in springtime and George and Simone have invited me for lunch. Their little apartment is at the end of the metro line but it is such a beautiful day that I take my chances and drive out in the Hillman.

It was one of those extraordinarily simple, tasty lunches that

French women manage with such seeming ease. Simone served us asparagus vinaigrette, that succulent spring asparagus we'd waited for all winter, followed by a trout, a crispy green salad (in which I can detect not the slightest hint of finely chopped liver of a chicken from Bresse but do detect a hint of mustard), some fine cheeses, and fruit. This has been put together in a minikitchen with no refrigerator, two burners, and a tiny oven, and served from one of those rolling carts on which clean plates arrive and empty plates are removed with no ado at all. The logistics are perfect.

George has a couple of wines he wants me to sample; sampling wines is one of our favorite indoor sports. We linger at the table into the afternoon, and it is then that George tells me about the great Pétain flap. This is a subject that cannot be mentioned in the presence of Robert Ahier, who played a leading role in the fiasco and who has never seen the humor of the situation, and I don't blame him.

It has become a famous newspaper story, told and retold with embellishments over the years. But this is how I first heard it from George who was there at the time although not himself involved.

The characters are:

Our own Robert Ahier.

Joe Grigg, the Paris bureau manager, a reddish-grey-haired Brit, with guardsman mustache and an Irish temper, a man who's been around the track.

The Kansas City milkman, a young American reporter just arrived from the States, extremely wet behind the ears, whose name no one ever remembers.

Marshal Philippe Pétain, hero of Verdun, villain of Vichy. Assorted French doctors, nurses, fishermen, and *tabac* owners.

It is 1951, and Pétain has contracted pneumonia in the Isle Yeu fortress prison off the wild Brittany coast. He is there under a life sentence. UP's front office is determined that United Press whip the opposition (AP) on Pétain's death, so they have authorized Grigg to spend whatever it takes to get the beat on Rox, which is the UP code word for Associated Press.

Grigg dispatches Ahier and Young American to the area. Robert, a fast talker who can be very persuasive, manages to get permission to visit the island. He suborns a fisherman into renting him his rowboat, which is against orders. Security on Isle Yeu is tightest, to use the agency jargon. Before leaving for Brittany, Ahier purchased a walkie-talkie and he has paid the owner of the tabac on the beach to put an out-of-order sign on his phone, the only public phone in that impossibly remote area.

The plan is as follows. Robert will return to the island, ingratiate himself with the nurses—he's a great hand with the ladies, he thinks. As soon as he hears that Pétain is dead he will row away from the island and flash his story to Young American, who will rush to the phone, tear off the out-of-order sign, drop in the *jeton* he has purchased in advance, and phone Paris, thus beating the rest of the world to the story. It is not a bad plan.

Robert takes up his vigil and in due course he sees two doctors emerge from Pétain's cell, shaking their heads. "*Mais, c'est fini*," says one. "*Le pauvre vieux*," says the other. This is all Robert needs. He rushes out. Gets into the rowboat. Paddles offshore. Mirabile dictu, the walkie-talkie works and Young American is still sober. Young American calls Paris. Grigg flashes PETAIN DEAD.

Rox is caught flat-footed.

Robert rows back to Yeu. But why is everything so calm? Why are people not charging around doing important things? Robert approaches a nurse, nervously, and asks when the funeral will be, and where? But the old man is not yet dead, she tells him. He's very sick, and may not live out the day, but one never knows, le bon Dieu will call him when the time is ripe.

Robert rows out and arouses Young American, who is waiting eagerly for the follow-up. "Paul," Robert says, "did you by any chance send out that story . . . ?"

The scene now shifts to the Paris bureau in its grubby quarters off the Boulevard des Italiens. George Sibera has just walked in. It is nearly an hour after the flash.

Joe Grigg is in the slot, a mound of torn copy paper at his feet, chewing a paper clip. He tears a sheet of paper out of his typewriter:

ISLE YEU, FRANCE (UP)—Marshal Phillippe Pétain, victor of Verdun, betrayer of France, was pronounced dead today.

It hits the floor, joining other discarded copy. Meanwhile the bells are ringing. It is probably Earl Johnson himself demanding the follow-up. Grigg chews another paper clip. Finally, says Sibera, Grigg heaves a great sigh, rolls another book in the battered Royal, and writes:

ISLE YEU, FRANCE (UP)—Doctors pronounced Phillipe Pétain, Marshal of France, dead at 2:04 this afternoon. But the heart of the gallant victor of Verdun refused to give up, and a minute later, started beating again.

At this point George slipped out, phoned Robert, and suggested that he not return to work for a week or so until tempers cooled. Young American was probably fired.

One Spring Morning

It's around 6:15, which is just about dawn these days when I step out the front door. The gaslight in the long lovely carriage-type street lamps we have on Eugène Delacroix suddenly stands out starkly outlined against the lightening sky with the entrancing roofs and chimneys of Paris behind them. All the concierges up and down the street are hurrying out in their bathrobes to pull in the garbage pails because a city ordinance requires they be inside within half an hour after the garbage collection is made. Ahmed, the Moroccan overnight man at the garage, is out in front smoking a companionable cigarette with a blue-clad street cleaner whose twig broom rests easily in the crook of an elbow. The little streams of water, negotiating their way around dams fashioned of rags, are trickling down the gutters, bearing old cigarette butts and shreds of paper to the drains.

We exchange good mornings and the street cleaner asks if I will be brave enough to drive to work today. The vicissitudes of my vehicle are a good-natured neighborhood joke. Ahmed grins and disappears into the garage to bring out the Hillman. The greengrocer from around the corner with the Chinese-long fingernails and the angora sweater he wears winter and summer, and the twin of which his wife seems perpetually to be knitting in the back of their store, picks up his truck for the early morning visit to Les Halles, the central Paris market, to gather the day's fruit and vegetables. He promises to save a good head of lettuce for me.

I drive down the Avenue Henri Martin to the Trocadéro, down Avenue Woodrow Wilson, and hit the Seine at the Place de l'Alma. Every day in the last fortnight as I have made this trip to report for the 7 A.M. shift the sky has become a smidgen lighter. Now it is almost full daylight. I drive past le Grand Palais and just beyond it am clipped by a truck driver barreling across the Alexandre III bridge, trying to beat a light. It is the lightest of tocs, a nudge really, and given the battered appearance of my unloved Hillman, I simply wave a forgiving wave at the driver and proceed on my way. At the Place de la Concorde, where the red light is prolonged, I look up to find a large mustached man at the window. I roll it down. It is the truck driver. He leans into the car, busses me on both cheeks, and returns to his truck in time to catch the green light. I'm greatly amused and can't wait to tell Danny Halperin about it.

I park on a side street off the Boulevard des Italiens. At this hour parking places aren't easy to find and I'm resigned to the ticket I get every month or so. I go to my usual morning bistro to find the grill only halfway up. Usually at this hour it is bustling with overnight workers coming in for their morning coffee and croissant, or a shot of black Martinique rum.

I bend down to look inside and a waiter tells me to come on

in. He explains that it is their *fermeture annuelle*, their month-long vacation, and they are cleaning up prior to their departure. The chairs are bunched on the tables and a waiter is mopping the floor. They offer to fill my thermos, as they do every morning, but there are no rolls or croissants. They refuse payment because, after all, they are *en vacance*. I wish them a happy vacation, and we shake hands all around.

It's ten minutes of seven when I get out of the elevator and elbow the door open. Danny is in his accustomed position in the slot, typing something. He waves in welcome, and finishes the story while I get out two cups, pour our coffee, and unwrap the croissants I bought at another bistro. It's a morning ritual, this, a comradely fifteen minutes in which Dan catches me up on what's going on and his small overnight adventures and contretemps, usually with the London bureau.

"Hey, Pitts," he says. "How about this?" And he carefully pulls from the spike a service message that came in overnight from London.

I N507 ƧⱲⱯ ⱤⱮ
27041 HALPERIN PLEASE TELL BUCKLEY HER MURDERED
CATHEDRAL WAS PRETTY AND DELICATE WRITING IN
OPINION OF LN ONITE DESK.
WILLARD
WD0619

I am inordinately pleased. What we usually get from LN (London) or NX (New York) are brickbats, not bouquets.

I had spent the prior weekend in Normandy with my friend Mina Wheeler and put up overnight at a small inn in Rouen,

In Rouen, they call it 'the murdered cathedral.'

Normandy's bustling capital city with its enchanting old town that Allied bombers badly mangled but failed to obliterate in the massive bombardments that preceded D-Day. Most severely damaged had been the ancient cathedral whose spires Joan of Arc saw when they carried her out to her execution pyre five hundred years earlier. The local people and press had been full of the story of *"la cathédrale meurtrisée,"* as they called it, "the murdered cathedral."

The first major Mass in ten years was to be performed in the now reconstructed murdered cathedral the following Sunday. It had taken ten years to stitch the cathedral back together, to restore its delicate Renaissance stone tracery and replace the sturdy gargoyles, pillars, and buttresses of an earlier period. "Here a pillar has been rebuilt from top to bottom," I had written. "Out there a stone carving from the hands of some unknown twelfth-century master is delicately joined to an ogival arch. At one side of the nave is a Corinthian column complete in every detail. Its twin was carved in 1252 A.D."

During the four years of the German occupation Rouen's

famous carillon had remained silent, master bell ringer Maurice Lenfant refusing to play for the Nazis. When liberating troops marched into a still smoking Rouen on August 31, 1944, they found the martyred cathedral half leveled, the supporting buttresses on its south side blown away, but from the battered medieval Tower of Butter, the carillon rang out loud and clear in the stirring strains of "La Marseillaise," and from the lacework spire the tricolor of France rippled in the hot summer air.

D-Day, Plus Ten

A year earlier I would have told everyone in the office that I would be visiting friends in Normandy, hard by the invasion beaches, over the June 6 weekend. But by this time I had learned a thing or two about United Press. Had I mentioned the visit, the editor would have suggested that since I was there anyway (and since this would entail no expenses for UP) why didn't I just file a story or two about the tenth anniversary D-Day celebrations, perhaps covering President Coty's tour of the invasion beaches and adding any sidebars that might be of interest. I would be on assignment, not on vacation.

So mum it was. I had a whole second day off on this particular weekend as a reward for an unscheduled Stakhavonite performance a couple of weeks earlier. There had been a major governmental crisis that went on late into the night and early the next morning before the current government either won its vote of confidence or lost it, I can't remember which. These crises occurred every three or four months in the Fourth Republic and we tended to roll with them.

At any rate, much of the staff had been covering the story from all sorts of angles since the afternoon before. When I reported for the 10 A.M. to 6 P.M. shift, Bill Landrey asked me to work a double shift because Sibera, who was scheduled for the six to midnight, had been up all the previous night. Fine, I said, no problem. But at midnight there was a problem. My replacement, I can't remember who he was, but it wasn't Danny Halperin, didn't show. I called around to his apartment, no answer, to a favorite restaurant, and so on. He wasn't to be found. So I hunkered down and wrote the routine overnighters and handled whatever else needed doing, including a rugby game or two.

By 7 A.M. I was bushed and sauntered to the bulletin board where the week's assignments were posted to find that it was I who was scheduled to replace the no-show overnight man. When Landrey loped in around eleven he was aghast to find me still in the slot, and was filled with such remorse that he promised me an extra day off whenever I wanted it. Before going off I checked the spike and found that I had filed 248 takes in the twenty-five hours or so I'd been alone in the office. (We wrote our stories in one-and two-paragraph segments, or "takes," so that the wire could be swiftly cleared when more urgent stories came through.)

When Antoinette de Berenger had asked me to spend the D-Day weekend at her home at St. Côme de Fresné, just a headland away from the Arromanches beachhead, I had accepted with pleasure and put in for the extra day. June 6, D-Day, was on Sunday in 1954. Antoinette worked at the U.S. Embassy and was a good friend of Mina's. We had had three or four suppers together and I much enjoyed her company.

Mina's car was "marching" that particular weekend, and the Seine valley between Paris and the coast sparkled with the bright and varied greens of the early summer. We arrived at St. Côme in mid-afternoon after a leisurely lunch en route. Antoinette had told us that her father was the mayor of St. Côme de Fresné, a village so tiny that his phone number was 1.

We arrived upon a scene of great agitation. M. le maire and his councilors were in informal session in the de Berenger living room. A crisis of unimaginable proportions had arisen. The presidential cortège was scheduled to sweep through St. Côme at 10:32 A.M. precisely the following morning. A president of France had not been in the town in the twentieth century, and perhaps not in the nineteenth. But tomorrow he would be here, and was the town prepared to receive him with the honor he deserved? No. No, no, no.

The children had been rehearsed. They would stand with the schoolmaster in front of the *mairie*, the city hall, each with his small tricolor, and as the presidential car swept past they would wave their flags and cry, in unison, "Vive la République," "Vive la liberation," and the schoolmaster would bow. On the balcony above their heads would be M. le maire, the abbé of l'Eglise St. Pierre, and other village elders. But the huge red, white, and blue flag that would complete the prescribed décor, draped over the balcony, was not to be found. They had searched everywhere. No one could remember when last it had been used, but whoever had used it had not put it away in its proper place. What a disgrace that St. Côme, of all the local villages, could not welcome the president of the Republic as he should be welcomed. They would never hear the end of it.

Vive la République!
Vive Mlle. Danton!

M. de Berenger barely had time to greet us before turning back to the crisis. Finally, one councilor suggested that perhaps Mlle. Danton might be persuaded to lend her flag to the mairie for the occasion. The assembled gentlemen seemed dubious about this possibility, knowing Mlle. Danton well as they did. And when it was suggested to M. de Berenger that he call Mlle. Danton, he was most reluctant to do so.

We understood why a moment later. The conversation was distinctly one-sided, and an irate Mlle. Danton could be heard all over the room. Why did M. le maire think she kept a large flag in her mother's mothproofed chest, if not for use when the president of the Republic came to town? Why did she take it out once a year and wash and press it? How could they expect to borrow her treasured tricolor when they, irresponsible men that they were, were so careless as to misplace the flag in the first place? And not to have made sure it was available when they first heard that the president would pass through St. Côme a month ago?

M. le maire got very few words in edgewise or any other way. But as so often in France the situation which, *en principe*, was hopeless, yielded to certain ingenious accommodations. And so it was that not precisely at 10:32 A.M. but more exactly at 11:50 the following morning when President René Coty's calvacade, which was running late, flashed through St. Côme,

there were the mayor and the parish priest and the local digni-
taries, including Mlle. Danton, on the balcony, above the children and the schoolmaster, all waving their little banners, but
the balcony they stood on was not the balcony of the mairie
but that of Mlle. Danton's handsome residence down the
street, and the balcony was adorned with a large, clean, well-
pressed *bleu, blanc, et rouge*. Vive la République. Vive Mlle.
Danton.

Antoinette's D-Day Tour

Sunday morning I inquired, a trifle hesitantly, about Mass.
One was never sure that French Catholics took their Sunday
obligations all that seriously. But Antoinette assured me that
both she and her parents were regular communicants and that
there was a ten o'clock Mass in a neighboring chapel. As the
hour neared and we sat about the living room chatting in
desultory fashion and reading the papers, Antoinette sensed
my restlessness. Don't worry, she said, I have my eye out for M.
le curé. And indeed a few minutes later, shortly after ten, we
spotted the priest, his soutane tucked up out of reach of the
wheels, a black beret on his head, bicycling rapidly up the hill
from the town. "We'll give him ten minutes," said Antoinette,
"to open up the church, light the candles, and get into his
vestments." Mme. de Berenger gave the marching orders by
putting on her hat and gloves and the three de Berengers and
their two American house guests heard Mass in the tiny
chapel on the hill behind the mayor's house, joining a congregation of fifteen or twenty souls.

That afternoon, with the hullabaloo of the ceremonies over, Antoinette took us on a private tour of the battlefields and beaches, explaining how the battle had developed with impressive mastery. She had been a young girl on that exciting day when the sea was black with ships and the skies silver and grey with planes and the Allied armies had swarmed ashore into Hitler's Fortress Europe. There was very little she didn't know about the climactic battles that had leveled a great deal of her beloved Normandy. She had never recovered from the exhilaration of those early days when the fate of the invading forces hung in the balance and her recital stirred the blood.

Late in the afternoon we visited a military cemetery: hundreds of white crosses marching in seried ranks down toward the sea from which they had come, each cross carrying the name, rank, and military outfit of the fallen soldier, a general buried next to a private in the democracy of the grave. We stood there, silent, with the clutch in the heart that military cemeteries always evoke, and said a prayer.

Driving back to St. Côme, I told Mina and Antoinette of my brother John's experience in Normandy during the war. It was in December of 1944 and John, who had served for eighteen months in North Africa, was on a week's leave in London. It was Christmas Eve and he was disporting himself at a night club popular with American servicemen when a couple of MPs walked in and called for the mike. They read out a list of names, John's among them, and announced that these officers' leaves had been canceled. The MPs then drove the men, they were all first and second lieutenants, to their billets to pick up their belongings and from there to an embarkation port where they were loaded onto a troop transport for France. There were 169 lieutenants in all. This was at the height of the Battle of the Bulge and replacements were urgently needed in the Ardennes.

Once in France, John and four other lieutenants climbed into a jeep with orders to report at once to military headquarters in Paris for reassignment. It was cold. Frigid, and two o'clock of a Christmas morning. They were a thoroughly dispirited group of young men, most of them still wearing the light raincoats they had started out in for what they had thought would be a festive evening on the town. As they drove along, John spotted a farmhouse with lights burning. He told the driver to pull up to it. Most Norman farmers made their own Calvados. Perhaps they could buy a couple of bottles to help ward off the cold.

John knocked on the door. A farmer opened it and asked gruffly what they wanted. John said they'd like to buy two bottles of Calvados. What kind of money did they have? John explained that all they had were British pounds. The farmer started to slam the door, but John put his boot in the jamb and held it open. We have cigarettes, he told the farmer, confident that that would turn the trick since American cigarettes were, at that time as good as, or even better than, currency.

"I don't smoke," said the farmer in a surly voice, and again tried to slam the door, but John's foot was still in the way. John is a peaceable man at most times, but he saw red at the farmer's churlish response, pulled out his pistol, and announced: *"Monsieur, de ce moment, vous êtes fumeur."* ("Sir, from this moment you are a smoker.") The deal was concluded, two bottles of Calvados in exchange for two cartons of Camels.

I had a feeling that Mina enjoyed the story rather more than did Antoinette.

Thirty years later, on the fortieth anniversary of D-Day, President and Mrs. Ronald Reagan visited those same beaches we had toured that afternoon, those same battlefields, the escarpment the Rangers had carried, the famous hedgerows, the graves. While the president took care of the official duties, Nancy Reagan was taken on a private tour of the impressive D-Day Museum and of some of the beaches. The story was covered at some length in the *New York Times*. Mrs. Reagan's guide, the *Times* reported, was the curator of the D-Day Museum, Mademoiselle Antoinette de Berenger.

I clipped the story and wrote Antoinette, hoping that the old St. Côme de Fresné address would still be applicable. She wrote right back, so very happy to hear from me after all these years and told me that she had moved home to Normandy in the early sixties to take care of her aging parents who were increasingly unable to cope. She had gotten a job with the group that was planning a museum to celebrate Operation Overlord, and in due course, when the museum was completed, had been invited to take over as curator. She added a postscript. I would be glad to know that she was still regularly attending the morning Mass that was occasionally said at ten these days since the new curé rode a *vélo*. Her parents were, I suspected, buried in the small graveyard by the chapel, as was the old curé.

The Bourgeois Presidency of René Coty

One felt that the very last thing René Coty had ever wanted or expected was to be elected president of France, but elected he was as a compromise candidate, the last president of the ram-

shackle Fourth Republic, making way for de Gaulle and the
Fifth Republic in 1959. He and his wife were the epitome of *le
petit bourgeois*, and when told that among his official duties
would be to host massive hunts in the Rambouillet Forest for
the likes of Prince Philip and Prince Bernhard of the Nether-
lands, Coty commented that the only thing he had ever shot in
his life was a crow, and that he had felt bad about it. It was with
the utmost reluctance that he and Mme. Coty took up residence behind the impressive black and gold ironwork gates of
the Elysée Palace. Whenever they could they escaped back to
their little walk-up apartment and had a Mme. Coty home-
cooked meal. Great was the scorn with which they were treated
by Paris sophisticates, but in their very simplicity and their
openness about their humble roots, they touched a chord that
was missed by both the local and the international press.

It came as a tremendous surprise to everyone when Mme.
Coty, suddenly stricken by what proved to be a fatal illness,
was moved to the hospital one night and was soon dead. Her
body would lie in state for twenty-four hours in the church of
La Madeleine, a prospect that would have dismayed her in life
but which she was powerless to prevent.

Mlle. Henri, our receptionist, was a woman of unchanging
habits. She walked in the door at precisely eight o'clock every
morning. At precisely twelve o'clock noon, she removed herself from the switchboard, tied into it whichever of the desks,
American or French, was at that moment in her disfavor,
walked to the back of the room with her lunch basket, and
refused to acknowledge anyone's presence for the next forty
minutes, before returning to the switchboard.

Thus it was with the greatest curiosity that I noted on this particular day Mlle. Henri put on her coat at noon and leave the office. It was almost an hour before she returned.

I asked her where she had been. She had walked down to the Madeleine to pay her final respects to Mme. Coty, she told me. En route she had picked up a bunch of violets at a flower stand. It was well known that violets were Mme. Coty's favorite flower, a humble flower to befit her unpretentious personality. When she got to the Madeleine, Mlle. Henri told me, she was astonished by the size of the crowd. A line stretched halfway around the block to the back of the church. She joined it and when she entered the basilica the scent was overpowering. There were, she said, thousands and thousands of small bouquets of violets spilling over the coffin and onto the floor, the gifts of the people of Paris.

"What kind of people?" I asked. "*Bien*," responded Mlle. Henri, "*des gents, quoi, comme moi. Des gents simples.*" People like me, simple folk.

Bastille Day

It's a little after nine at night before I leave the bureau. I park the Hillman near the Louvre and walk halfway across le Pont Royal, pausing to watch the fireworks. Every monument in Paris is illuminated tonight—Bastille Day—and the crowds are in a festive mood. As the sky lights up in showers of rose and green, a little girl sitting on the railing, her father's arms holding her tight, murmurs over and over. "*Oh, papa, que c'est beau. Que c'est beau, papa, que c'est beau.*" Her enthusiasm delights the crowd.

Oh, papa, que c'est beau.

I cross to the far bank and walk up the Rue du Bac to the Boulevard St. Germain and down toward the Place St. Germain which is where the action is tonight. The police have cordoned off a huge segment on the Left Bank, three or four street bands are playing on the Place. Tables and chairs have been brought out into the street and the local bars, Les Deux Magots, Brasserie Lipp, and the Flore are doing a landslide business, perspiring waiters rushing back and forth with full bottles of wine and giant mugs of beer. People are dancing in the street, laughing, smoking, talking, arguing, having the best of times on this cool and clement midsummer evening. Once in a while, a band, remembering the occasion for this jollity, strikes up "La Marseillaise," a signal for everyone, French and foreign, to rise and join the stirring chorus: *"Allons, enfants de la Patrie, le jour de gloire est arrivé."*

Nick King spots me across the square and we join in the

dancing, the pavement rough under our feet but, *zut alors*, this is Paris, this is Bastille Day. A tall, slender young man breaks in, introduces himself, and asks me to dance. I don't catch his name in the general uproar but we whirl about for a jig or two, and when the band takes a break he invites me to join his group for a glass of wine. We move to a crowded table. Someone brings over an extra chair and I find myself talking to a quite stunning American woman, her dark hair drawn back in a severe bun that accentuates her classic profile. She is the wife of the young man who has danced with me. His name is Broadwater. She is Mary McCarthy, the author. They are friends of, and I believe he is in some way related to, Nick King.

Everyone I know in Paris seems to be out on this festive night. Dan Halperin introduces us to his date. She comes from Martinique; her perfect French has a Caribbean cadence to it which we find charming. They have Ed Cornish in tow. Ed is the most recent member of the team, transferred almost overnight from Rome to fill a large hole in the staff caused with the disappearance of three key men. Ed Korry has been named foreign editor of *Look* magazine to replace Bill Attwood there. Ken Miller has been reassigned to London to fill the news editor slot and Bob Rigby—refused a raise—has quit to try his hand at freelancing. Bob figures the wages will be about the same, if less regular, but the hours much better. As a married man with two young sons, the six-day week and irregular working hours are more discommoding to him than to us single folk.

Ed Cornish, who is fluent in Italian, is less so in French although learning fast. He's a slight young man with short curly blond hair, a boyish look behind heavy horn-rimmed glasses. Ahier has instantly nicknamed him *"cornichon"* (pickle), and the nickname is sticking. Behind the bland countenance is an imaginative first-class brain and fine news sense. He will end up, some years later, after a stint with *National Geographic*, as president of the World Futurist Society. Eddie and I will see quite a lot of each other after we both return to the States.

It's about 2 A.M. when Nick walks me back to my car. All is quiet in the dank narrow streets that lead from St. Germain back to the Seine although the bands are still at it at the Place St. Germain. Just beyond the Rue de l'Université one little tabac is still in business, however, a cloud of blue-grey smoke billowing into the street from the doors that have been flung open to take advantage of the early morning breeze. The jukebox blares out a country-western ditty with the unlikely refrain on this night of celebration to the French Revolution of 1789: "Old Joe Stalin. You're eating too high on the hog."

All is quiet in the dank streets that lead from St. Germain to the Seine.

We laugh, tickled by the lunacy of it all. I suddenly remember and tell Nick that it was a quarter-century ago, on another Bastille Day, in the American hospital in Neuilly, that my mother gave birth to my redheaded youngest brother Reid. Fireworks were bursting all over Paris the night Reid came into the world, and he's been setting them off ever since.

A Riotous Morning

Arthur Higbee, our newest bureau chief, calls me at home. There is a twenty-four-hour civil servant strike—it is the postal workers this time—and the authorities fear there might be violence. Could I drive to work via the Boulevard Haussmann, near St. Augustin, where the strikers are demonstrating and see if anything newsworthy is going on?

No problem at all. I swing left at the Grand Palais toward the *rond-point,* to hit Haussmann not far from St. Augustin. On a small street a couple of blocks short of the avenue two blue police vans are parked with tough riot police seated inside. They are there obviously to lend a hand if the situation becomes too difficult for the regular police to handle. These are no-nonsense hombres, not to be trifled with.

My Hillman is in a balky mood this morning, threatening to stall at every red light, and a stall is a terrifying thing opening up as it does the possibility of a dread démarreur coincé. I play with the clutch and the gas pedal as I turn onto a boisterous Avenue Haussmann. The strikers are all over the place, but so far the police have been able to keep the traffic moving, if at a crawl, pushing the demonstrators back onto the sidewalks when they threaten to march on the avenue itself. I mosey along slowly. Nothing much to report, at least right now. And then there is the most frightful explosion. It's taking place under the hood of my car. A banging and crashing. Steam envelops the entire front of the car. A policeman turning quickly to see what the commotion is about knocks a striker into the street inadvertently. A second striker grabs the policeman. Another *flic* runs to help his comrade, and before you know it there are men wrestling and cuffing each other all over the street. Meanwhile the steam continues to pour out from under the hood of the Hillman. Several times I start to open the door but figure I'm safer inside than out unless something starts to burn. Finally, the fighting lets up enough for me to get out, and I head back a couple of blocks to a garage I had spotted when I made the turn into Haussmann. (If one drives a car like mine, one is always keeping one's eyes out for possible garages because one never knows when one will need them.)

I explain my predicament, and a mechanic is dispatched to accompany me back to the car to see what can be done. The mechanic opens up the hood and finds the problem at once. The bolt that keeps the water hose fastened to the radiator has given way. The banging and crashing I had heard was the bolt rattling around under the hood. The boiling water from the radiator, hitting the hot engine, had caused the steam.

The situation can easily be remedied once the Hillman is in the garage. The mechanic tells me he'll be back in a few minutes with a tow truck. What he arrives in is not a tow truck but a dilapidated Peugeot sedan. He pulls ahead of the Hillman and attaches the Hillman to the Peugeot with a short metal bar, three or four feet long. He tells me to get back into the driver's seat and release the brake but not to touch the wheel, and we start slowly out. The police and the strikers are no longer fighting, but heady words are being exchanged. A brawny mailman rushes toward a cop to make a verbal point at closer quarters, fails to note the iron bar that has attached my slowly moving Hillman to the car ahead, catches his toe on it, and sprawls into the street, and the riot is resumed. Three or four more times someone trips over the same rod, none of them noting that the

Peugeot and Hillman are engaged in a *pas de deux*. Just like that, I have managed to set off my second riot of the morning.

It's No Joke

Dick George, a young American doctor doing the equivalent of his residency at the American Hospital in Neuilly, cannot understand why Mina and I put up with the vagaries of our cars. Dick received a gorgeous red Buick convertible from his parents as a graduation-from-medical-school gift, and he has it here in Paris. It is both the love of his life and the bane of his existence. It looks huge compared to most French cars. What Dick fears is a fender bender with one of those crazy frogs whose only purpose when they get behind the wheel, he believes, is to maim the opposition. Dick will go miles out of his way in order not to have to drive around the Arch of Triumph, which is to Paris drivers the ultimate test of their virility. Every morning he rushes from his breakfast to the street where the Buick is parked to check that the fenders have survived one more night of perilous Paris parking.

He counts the days until his two-year stint will be up and he can remove his treasure to the safety of American streets. Against all odds, the Buick survives its Parisian tour. After a round of farewell parties, for Dick is very popular with our group, he drives to Cherbourg and sees his car aboard the ocean liner that will bring them both home. In New York he waits in the drafty customs shed for several hours until the car is off-loaded, gets behind the wheel, and starts up Tenth Avenue singing a happy song. At the first red light he is rammed from the rear, bang, crash, thud, and he is still shaking from the shock of the encounter when the driver of the offending car rushes up to him and says: *"Pardonnez-moi, monsieur. Je m'excuse. C'est ma faute."*

The Moroccan Restoration

In the late nineteenth and early twentieth centuries France established her rule over the Maghreb, the three nations bordering the southern flank of the western Mediterranean: Tunisia, which grew out of the ruins of ancient Carthage, Algeria, and along the Atlantic coast, Morocco. The natives were becoming increasingly restive in the liberation fever that followed the Second World War, and in an effort to head off trouble, France made a deal with El Glaoui, the fierce chieftain of the Berber tribesmen in the Rif Mountains, to oust the Moroccan king, Sultan Muhammad V, who was proving fractious, and to exile him in plush but well-guarded quarters on a French Pacific island. The young sultan was free to do just about anything he wanted except leave the island.

But now things were changing. El Glaoui was in his eighties and less of a threat, and it seemed advisable to French authorities to make their peace with the young king and restore him to his throne where, it was hoped, he would continue to cooperate with France. El Glaoui was given what amounted to marching orders and it was arranged that he would make his obeissance to the sultan in a ceremony at the Château de St. Cloud just outside Paris. I was sent to cover the story and arrived just too late to get into the large and ornate hall in which the scene was to be enacted. But the *Time* magazine man, Frank White, and I managed to get a spot by an open window from which we could watch the show.

The sultan was seated in a large upholstered chair on a small platform. At the given signal the doors opened and in came El Glaoui, still tall, still erect in his striped Berber robes, his head held high. Eighty years of desert sun and winds had turned his skin to mahogany. He had a prominent fierce eagle nose and fierce eyes to match. He strode down the hall toward the young king, and as he reached him bent his knee creakily as an old man does no matter how proud he is, and started to kneel in order to kiss the sultan's shoe in a sign of his surrender. But before he could complete the maneuver, the young king rose, grabbed the old man by the elbows, raised him up, and embraced him. It was a gracious gesture, all the more so because it was unexpected, and from the crowded room there were murmurs of approval and a scattering of applause.

I hurried to the nearest phone, called in a bulletin to the desk, and dictated five or six paragraphs of the story before rushing back to the office to write the night lead.

It was with considerable surprise three or four days later, while flipping through *Time* magazine, that I read that when El Glaoui had started to kneel, Muhammad V had leaned over and roughly pushed the old man's head down to the floor. I called Frank. "That's not how I saw it," I told him. Nor, he told me, was that how he had seen it, either. He had written the same version of the story as I had, but in New York some editor apparently had decided it would make a more dramatic story if the king bashed El Glaoui, and so emended Frank's copy. Frank was less indignant than I would have been, because this kind of thing happened to *Time* and *Newsweek* correspondents so often. Back in the fifties, bylines were rare in the news magazines; news was gathered in the field, but it was shaped for publication by a staff of editors and rewrite men in New York. I was shocked and conveyed that shock to Nick, who, like Frank, was not at all surprised by my story. He had seen it happen too often, but he didn't like it any more than I did.

The Quai d'Orsay, as it turned out, had pulled off a brilliant maneuver with Muhammad V's restoration. The sultan died five or six years later and today, a good fifty years later still, Muhammad's grandson rules in Rabat, the nearest thing to an absolute monarch anywhere in the world. Morocco and France remain friends and allies.

Musical Brouhaha

Mina Wheeler's cousin Geoffrey Crawford was cultural attaché at the U.S Embassy. He asked me one evening when we were having a drink at Mina's whether I knew anything of Edgard Varèse. The name drew a blank. Geoff told me that Varèse had been an avant-garde composer back in the twenties, and that he was in fact so avant-garde that today, in the fifties, his music was still not accepted and was only rarely performed.

Varèse, who had lived in the United States for some years, had been invited by a French impresario to present one of his compositions at a concert the following weekend and Geoff wondered if United Press would be interested in covering the concert. That was not the kind of thing that UP generally covered, I told Geoff. Would I be interested in writing something about Varèse? he asked. No way, I said. I didn't know enough about music to write a critique of "A long long trail a-winding" let alone an avant-garde composition that even real musical critics didn't understand. But Geoff was insistent. Washington had asked him to do something to get coverage of Varèse's concert.

Would I like to meet Varèse? Geoff persisted. He was a terribly nice man and I would enjoy talking to him. And so it was that two days later I found myself walking into a second-class hotel near the Gare Montparnasse. Varèse met me at the third-floor elevator and we went down the hall to his small corner room. The composer was probably in his early seventies at the time. He had longish wiry speckled grey and white hair, wore a plaid wool shirt buttoned at the neck and worn brownish corduroy trousers fastened about a broad waist with a heavy brown belt. He wore socks and sandals and a most enchanting smile.

He was so pleased that I had agreed to see him, and thought it would be useful if I looked over some of his scrapbooks, which he had open on the bed. They contained newspaper clippings, most of them a quarter-century old, and most of them bitterly critical of the electronic music that Varèse had pioneered in his search for what he called "organized sound." His compositions had names like *Hyperprism* and *Arcana* and *Ionisation*, this last a piece for percussion instruments that was to be performed at the Salle Pleyel (I think it was the Pleyel) the following Saturday night.

I made a few notes, things I thought might be useful if I could figure out a news angle for the story, and Varèse then invited me to walk to a nearby café for refreshments. We walked up and down a few quiet side streets in search of a particular bistro he was anxious to show me. As we walked he pointed out architectural details on the buildings we passed and told me wonderful stories of his years as a student of Debussy in

Paris following World War I. He
was a genial host and most disap-
pointed that he couldn't find the
bistro he was looking for because
there were in the back room price-
less paintings by Miró, Matisse,
Picasso, and many others, that the
kindhearted patron had taken in
lieu of cash from the impoverished
young artists who frequented his
café. It was nowhere to be found.
But the day was pleasant, and we
were both enjoying our stroll. At a
small street flower stand Varèse
bought me a bunch of violets and

At a street flower stand Varèse
bought me a bunch of violets.

we ended up at the Dôme where he had a beer and I a cup of
coffee. He was sorry that his wife, the talented French-English
translator Louise Varèse, was not there to meet me. She was in
London talking to her publisher.

I told Mr. Varèse that I was not equipped to write musical
criticism but he insisted that what he wanted was a simple news
story about his return to the city of his youth for the first concert there in many a year. He asked me if I would attend the
concert and I said that of course I would. It would be a pleasure.

I went with Mina and the Crawfords. Someone in the host
organization must have had it in for Varèse because the first
piece on the program that night was Tchaikovsky's Sixth Sym-
phony, the *Pathétique,* which is melodic in the extreme. An
audience warmed up by the Tchaikovsky was then served up
Edgard Varèse's *Ionisation.* The violins and horns and cellos

made way for a stage full of percussionists. It is hard to describe the sounds that next assailed our untutored ears. It was a rhythmic din embroidered with recorded bits of jackhammers and police sirens and other street noises. The audience listened intently for about ten minutes, then someone got up and shouted that this wasn't music, and he wouldn't listen to it. Someone shouted at him to shut up and let them hear the composition out. There were catcalls. People stamped their feet. "It's an obscenity," someone yelled. "Quiet," roared someone else. "I want to hear it." Here and there men struggled to be heard. The musicians finally gave up as much of the audience, including us, headed for the exits. The police sirens we now heard came from the street outside the hall where the police were responding to what looked like a riot. It was obvious that no more music was to be performed in that hall that night. As we made our way out, Geoff commented: "I knew the French could be this rude. But I didn't know they cared this much."

It made for a grand story, which turned out to be a United Press exclusive. I sent Geoff a copy and he reported back that Edgard Varèse had been delighted with it. That pleased me because he was a gentle lovely man whose music I would never understand, or like, but whose courage and dedication I admired. And whose violets had touched me.

But Which Archangel?

NEWS STORIES are to be found everywhere. While going through *France-Soir*, the big Parisian afternoon paper one day, my eye was caught by a picture of a *clochard*, one of the ubiquitous ragpickers who are as much a part of the Paris scene as the *bouquinistes* on the quais of the Seine. It was a brief color piece about a tramp who believed he was an archangel. What fascinated me was that I thought I knew this particular *archange*.

This was early on in my Paris UP career, while I was still living on the Rue Coypal, near the Place d'Italie. I'd taken, when driving home after finishing my 7 A.M. to 3 P.M. shift, to stopping at a little bar-tabac on the Boulevard des Italiens for a cup of coffee and a cigarette. Sometimes I'd read the paper, but mostly I'd just watch the people passing by, back and forth, and eavesdrop on their conversations. Occasionally, a clochard would be sitting on a bench in front of the café under the chestnut trees, his nondescript cloak wrapped closely around him, drinking in the warmth of the spring sun. Could this be the man mentioned in this morning's *France-Soir* story?

"My" clochard and I were on a chatting basis since I had some weeks earlier offered him a Camel after I saw him scavenge a half-smoked cigarette a passerby had dropped on the sidewalk. I was a little hesitant about offering him a cigarette, but he took it with a word of thanks and asked me for *un feu*, a light. Those small packets of matches so available for the taking in America were in short supply in postwar Paris. Everyone who smoked, and that was everyone you knew, carried a lighter. I took mine out, gave him a light. He thanked me again and we said good-bye. This became a routine.

Today, I stopped for a coffee hoping the archangel would be there, and to my joy he was.

"Well, monsieur," I said as I offered him the pack, "how does it feel to be so famous?" He wanted to know what I was talking about. Hadn't he seen the story in *France-Soir*? He had not. I retrieved the paper from my car and showed it to him. He read the item, slowly, carefully, and then commented that the reporter was a salopard, a dirty dog.

This was not the response I had expected. Look, look, he said, pointing a dirty finger toward one sentence in the story. "He calls me the Archangel Michael. Me! Michael! But I am not Michael."

"You're not the archangel?" I was confused.

"But of course I'm the Archangel. But I am the archangel Gabriel, the angel who informed the Palestinian maiden ever so gently that she would be the mother of God." Michael, he reminded me, was a bloodthirsty angel. It was Michael who had thrust Satan and all the evil spirits into Hell, where they would seek the damnation of souls; Michael who had barred with flaming sword the Garden of Eden to Adam and Eve after they had fallen from grace; Michael who had slain the dragon. "I, madame," he said, "am a archangel, but also a pacifist."

He asked if he could keep the clipping and I said that of course he could and that if he wished I could bring him a second copy tomorrow. But he smiled, pointed to the bundles at his feet, and reminded me that he had very little storage space. One copy would be fine. I smiled, and said good-bye, and for the first time we shook hands. It made a haunting rather pleasant little story for a dead news day.

I soon learned that it doesn't do to trifle with archangels, gentle or bloodthirsty however. Because for the next two or three months, whenever the news report was on the dull side, Paris would get a message from London suggesting it produce a story with "Buckley's archangel touch," and you can guess who got the assignment.

Une Maison un Peu Bizarre

Sometimes a story hits you over the head and demands to be told. Nick King and I had been covering a not very interesting press conference on riot control at the Palais de Justice. It was late afternoon when it broke up and Nick suggested that since we were on the Ile de la Cité it might be fun to have a drink at the new bar Ludwig Bemelmans had opened near Notre Dame. It was said to be charming. A gendarme gave us directions and soon we were stepping down a couple of steps into Bemelmans's bar. It was unlike other French bistros, both bright and airy, not musty and brown. The walls had been painted white and Bemelmans had covered them with murals. There were Madeline and her friends walking, two by two, down the steps in front of Sacré Coeur with Miss Clavell in anxious attendance. On the far wall was a major traffic jam a-building around a charmingly elongated Arc de Triomphe; you could almost hear the cacophony of the horns and the imprecations of the drivers. Here small boys with their mothers and nannies launched sailboats on the lake in the Tuileries gardens while off to the side a wicked child on a scooter snatched the beret off the head of a friend. One Paris street scene after another, all in unmistakable Bemelmans colors and shapes.

We sat down and ordered a *pichet* of Sancerre which the waiter highly recommended.

Minutes later the door shot open and in burst a stout middle-aged woman wearing sturdy walking shoes and serviceable lisle stockings, her shapeless body encased in a shapeless coat, oatmeal in color. It reminded us of Nancy Mitford's comment that the fine Scottish tweeds British aristocrats favored for country wear could be any color providing the overall effect was porridge.

There was no resemblance between British aristocrats and the woman now charging the bar. In a voice a drill sergeant would be proud of, she informed the bartender that she was an official representative of the French government engaged in the important task of taking the census. Would he like to see her credentials? It wouldn't be necessary, madame.

Was he the owner of this bistro? He was not, he was merely employed to tend bar. Who was the owner? He didn't know. How could he not know if he was employed here? The bartender explained patiently that the bar had been rented to a M. Bemelmans and that he was M. Bemelmans's employee. Was M. Bemelmans here? He was not. When would he be in? The waiter didn't know.

He hadn't been in for a couple of weeks and might well be in America. What would he be doing in America? The waiter explained that M. Bemelmans, who was an artist, and he pointed to the murals, was an American and lived in Paris only part of the year.

The woman took in the murals, made no comment, but shook her head as if to say, "What will these Americans think of next."

"Well," she said, "are there any other people living in this building?" There were, the bartender said, three apartments on the upper three floors and he believed they were occupied but he didn't know by whom. It was none of his business.

The census taker asked if she could leave her heavy briefcase and he motioned her to the table next to ours. "Place it there, madame," he said. "It will be quite safe." She thanked him, extracted a clipboard and some forms from it, put the briefcase on the table, and went off to pursue her search.

Fifteen minutes later she was back, bursting into the bar as explosively as she had the first time, and informed the bartender in stentorian tones that *"ici c'est une maison un peu bizarre!"* "This is a crazy house." She had pounded on the door of the first-floor apartment for quite five minutes and gotten no response so, *faute de mieux,* she had stuck a census form under the door with a note saying it was important, even imperative! that the locataire fill it out at once! And mail it, at once!

On the second floor she had found someone in, a woman. But was she the occupant of the flat? She was not! She was just there to help out a friend who had been called away suddenly on business by taking care of his cat and watering his plants. At least, the census taker conceded, she had known the name of the locataire, which was some little help. But did she know the date of his birth, and where he was born? Of course not! So she had left another form to fill out telling the woman that it was important, even imperative! that it be filled in at once!

On the third floor, she had been more successful. She had found a couple in, but, here she paused, a very important question had arisen: were they, as they claimed, man and wife? Heavy shrug. The explanation the woman had given was that she had kept her maiden name when she got married for professional reasons, but one wonders. Not, she added hastily, that it is the job of the official government census taker to make moral judgments. Her only job is to count people. Having now thoroughly ruined the reputation of the people on the third floor, she ordered a pot of tea and sat down to fill out her forms.

When she had left Nick asked me if I had noticed that the forms she carried came in both white and pastel shades. I had. "You know why?" he asked. Nick sops up information of this sort. It's one of the things that makes him such a good reporter. "It is so the French government will not insult its *brebis égarée*, its stray sheep. Nick had been reliably informed (by his concierge) that when a census taker suspected that the sweet little thing in M. Piccard's apartment might not be Mme. Piccard, he or she filled out the questionnaire on a pastel sheet, and on the great collation day, the pastel sheets were cross-checked with the white sheets. If it was found that two Guillaume Piccards had been born on the same day, November 24, 1925, in the same town, Provins (which is not a very big town), then one of the Guillaumes would not be included in the final count. Never let it be said that *la République* did not know the difference between census and censure. *Vive la délicatesse!*

The Palais de Justice Wants Me!

I'm in one mell of a hess. Upon my return from an emergency visit to South Carolina, where I had been summoned by my father's most serious stroke to date, I found in the accumulated mail a formidable pink document. It was a formal *convocation* from M. l'inspecteur Druoud to visit him at the Palais de Justice on August 10 at 10 A.M. If I failed to heed this summons an order for my arrest might be issued.

But this is August 16. I am already a week late. I call M. Beaupré for help and advice, but my Palais de Justice mentor is en vacance and will not return until September. I call Bill Landrey—he has replaced Ed Korry as bureau manager—but he is unfamiliar with French bureaucratic procedures and, while sympathetic, is of little help. Robert Ahier is gleeful. "Ah-ha, Peets," he says, "they have caught you out for changing your money on the black market." I suspect that Bob is right on this one. My papers are all in order. I have my authorization to practice journalism in France from the prime minister's office no less. I have duly signed in and out of precinct police stations as required by law when I have changed apartments. But in nearly two years I've never cashed a legal check. M. Michel in the *rez-de-chaussée* photography shop at 2 Rue des Italiens has been my only banker.

Only last week I had had a wonderful experience with M. Michel. My brother John had arrived in town with his wife Ann at the end of a European vacation and was short of cash. He was about to take off for American Express when I suggested he give me a check instead and I would cash it with M. Michel at a far better rate than he would get at Amex. The check was for $500. My usual transactions with M. Michel were in the $50 to $100 range. Yes, M. Michel would be delighted to cash a check of any brother of Mlle. Buckley. We retired to the back room where this, the major portion of M. Michel's business, was transacted and formally checked the morning *Herald Tribune* for the current rate of exchange. M. Michel pulled a large book in which he kept his ready cash out of the bookcase, but as he started to count out the hundreds and hundreds of French francs I noted a slowdown in the procedure. Something was bothering M. Michel. Finally he stopped counting and, looking a mite embarrassed, asked me confidentially, "How well do you know your brother?" Which translated into: "Is this check good?"

"Very well," I replied, "from the very day of my birth." M. Michel laughed nervously, and gave me the money.

A couple of phone calls to the Palais de Justice did nothing but compound my confusion. So Bill Landrey, obviously worried about the situation, suggested I go see Inspector Druoud at once, and explain why I was late in replying to his convocation. Bill was no help at all in suggesting how I would reply to any questions about my fiscal dealings while a guest of *la République*, but he could certainly confirm why I was late in reporting to M. Druoud.

So I trotted down to the Palais de Justice with my pink convocation in hand. I explained to numbers of bureaucrats why I was here on August 17 instead of the tenth. And was told to wait. And wait I did in office after office on those creaky collapsible chairs that are direct descendants of the iron maidens of more brutal ages. Much of the morning was spent moving from office to office, waiting my turn to be summoned by a bored official who would in due course send me to another office to bother yet another bored civil servant.

At noon the offices closed for two hours and I was ordered to report at 2 P.M. to an office on a higher floor where the inspectors were kept. I arrived back punctually and was actually called in by M. l'inspecteur Gilbert.

I told him why I was late. That was quite understandable he said and no problem. However, unfortunately, M. l'inspecteur Druoud was on vacation. What was it that he had wanted to see me about? I didn't know. "You have no idea?" (Well, I had some idea but I wasn't about to open up that can of worms.) M. Gilbert was helpful and far from frightening. Perhaps he could find Inspecteur Druoud's file. He pulled a chair over to the wall, picked out a dusty file drawer, brought it to his desk, and foraged in it for a few minutes.

He couldn't find anything about my case. He asked to see my convocation again. And then that blessed man tore it in two and said those blessed words: *"C'est annulée."* (It's canceled.)

I never heard from the Palais de Justice or Inspecteur Druoud again and continued cashing my checks with M. Michel
until the day I left Paris.

The High Livers of Cognac

Henry McFarland is a first-rate PR man with an inventive, merry
imagination. At the moment Mac is representing the cognac
industry. He calls and makes an enthusiastic pitch; his pitches
are always enthusiastic. He's running a weekend trip to Cognac
and he really wants me to join the group. It's a great story, "a
really great story, Pitts," he enthuses. Henry has discovered that
there are more people over one hundred years old in Cognac
than in any other geographic district in France of equal size.

"I suppose you're going to tell me that cognac is good for
your health," I start.

"Not at all. Not at all."

What the medical people have concluded—he tells me, and
I am only too ready to believe him under the circumstances—is
that it is inhaling the cognac fumes while
the wine is maturing in oaken casks that
has such a salutary effect on the longevity
of the locals. Much of the highly com-
bustible wine ages in long, low, open
sheds scattered around the countryside. The fumes emanating
from this gestating wine are
indeed strong enough to grow
a greenish fungus on the tin

You're going to tell me that
cognac is good for your health?

roofs of these sheds. It is this heady aroma, inescapable if you live in the Cognac region, that must account for the long lives of its people. *Voilà*. Anyway, that's his story and he intends to stick with it, as will I.

During the war, we are told in the course of the trip, the Germans who were no fools, and who knew there must be more wine maturing in the Cognac region than the natives had owned up to, were frustrated until one bright fellow commandeered a hot air balloon, and soon enough he spotted and mapped out those areas that stood out from the general brownish late August country-side by their greenish hue. Moreover these hues were mostly rectangular in shape. Sure enough, that was where the locals had dug pits for their wine when informed the Germans were coming to town. It was very sad, *une vraie calamité*, but fortunately the war ended before much of the wine had been confiscated.

The occasion for Mac's junket would be a municipal ceremony in which thirteen centenarians who were more or less ambulatory if not necessarily compos would be honored by the prefect and the cognac industry. The reception would culminate with the presentation to each honoree of a bottle of cognac that had been put down in the year of his birth.

An intriguing proposition, and anyway it would be a great deal of fun as were all of Henry McFarland's capers. (I had been on a couple, including one in which a dancer from the Folies Bergères had landed on a barge in the Seine from a helicopter to celebrate the discovery of a heretofore unpublished chapter by Rabelais in which Pantagruel recommends to his friends that when they drink champagne, they drink only the genuine article, champagne made in Champagne. Another of Henry's clients is the champagne industry.)

I accepted with the proviso that I would have to be back in Paris in time to work the 6 P.M. to midnight shift on Saturday. Art Buchwald had declined McFarland's invitation because the story would not be an exclusive. His reputation was such that he could get away with such demands, but Mac decided he would get more mileage out of the six who had accepted, two or three other agency people, and a fellow from the *Chicago Tribune*.

The leaves were turning yellow and gold as we neared Cognac itself, and the long lines of grapevines were green, yellow, and bright red. It had been a long drive from Paris, a bit over four hundred kilometers almost due south. We went directly to the fields—the *vendange* (harvest) was in progress—and watched the process from the pressing of the grapes to their transfer to the distillation rooms. A youngish man with an elongated hooked nose that would have made Cyrano proud shepherded us through the Hennessy plant. He and his father handled all of the tasting, which is a very complex procedure because good cognac is an amalgam of cognac wines of different qualities and years. Each type of cognac is mixed a minimum of ten times, and the object is to have every bottle of Three Star or of VSOP taste exactly like every other bottle of Three Star or VSOP. The taster told us that his grandfather had been a taster for Hennessy, as well as his great-grandfather and his great-grandfather's great-grandfather. He said he could taste up to eighty cognacs a day. He showed us how, swirling the wine in a deep sapphire, tulip-shaped wine glass so that the color would not affect his judgment. As he smelled it I wondered whether each generation of his family had developed a longer nose than the last, a finer instrument for the work at hand. Looking at him, it seemed not only probable but virtually certain. Then he spat the wine out into a huge leather basket filled with sawdust.

We were good and tired and ready for a break when we checked in at Hennessy House, a lovely mellow grey stone Renaissance town house where guests of the industry are lodged. It came complete with a most obliging resident staff. We were each ushered into a suite—bedroom, bathroom, sitting room—and instructed to leave out any shoes we would like polished or clothes to be pressed. Upon our merry return later that evening each one of us found a thermos of ice water and a small pitcher of cognac on his bedside table, which called for a continuation of festivities far into the night.

Then it was off to the centenarians' reception in the mairie. It is rather startling to enter a room with thirteen people over one hundred years old, but quite a few of them, five or six, were standing around glass in hand thoroughly enjoying life. One, he was 104, had been mayor of his town until two years earlier. Another handful sat quietly in their chairs and wheelchairs not taking very much in, but occasionally making the effort to smile and nod a bonnetted head. A pompous fellow with the ritualistic tricolor sash over the ritualistic bulging chest took the microphone and was intoning away when an old lady, one of the honored guests, shuffled forward in her felt slippers, seized the microphone from the astonished prefect, murmured in a shrill cackle that she could sing better than he could talk, and broke into a shrill rendition of "La Marseillaise." For a moment there was stunned silence. Then the crowd, tickled, joined in and all those who could were soon standing at attention and saluting the flag. The prefect never did get back the floor.

Then it was on to a huge oak-lined upstairs room in a local

restaurant, which the cognac industry uses for entertaining, and a splendid four-course dinner served by candlelight. I was vastly amused—I was the only woman along—to find myself sitting between, if you can believe it, M. Maurice Hennessy and M. Maurice Martell, and just across the table from M. Jean Rémy-Martin. The Hennessys, Martells, and Rémy-Martins have been operating in Cognac for two to three hundred years. M. Hennessy, who was perfectly charming, told me one of his ancestors was a British seaman who had been wrecked off the Bordeaux coast in the late seventeenth century, had swum ashore and ultimately married the farmer's daughter. Hence the name. Maurice Hennessy was a tall, handsome sunburned man of sixty or so with a crop of thick white hair cut short and the lightest of blue eyes. His English reflected his Oxford education. All of his family, he told me, had traditionally been sent back to the old country for their education.

Next morning we visited a working Rémy-Martin farm where a handful of aged carpenters was splitting by hand great logs cut from oaks in the Limousin forest, shaping them into barrel staves. M. Rémy-Martin explained that they don't use saws because the saw could break the grain of the wood and cause unnecessary evaporation of the maturing wine. The staves are then fitted together into barrels.

The old farmhouse was lovely, with quite exquisite oak paneling. In the huge old-fashioned kitchen they were roasting a whole lamb on a spit for lunch, but it was a lunch I would not taste because I had to catch a train that would get me back to Paris in time for my Saturday-night shift. M. Rémy-Martin was outraged that I couldn't stay long enough to taste the meal they were preparing for us. It was something very special, he said. A week or so later I received from him a beautiful scarf imprinted with the map of the Cognac country to make up, he had written in longhand, for the lunch I had missed. I wore it for years.

Max Blouet's Culinary Institute

Mostly I go to concerts with my friend Phebe Cates. Phebe is the older sister of David Cates who was a friend of my brother Bill's at Millbrook School. She is in Paris studying voice and David had asked her to look me up. Phebe is on top of the musical scene in Paris and calls from time to time to ask if I'd like to go to this or that concert. But in real life, to support herself, Phebe does public relations for the swanky George V hotel just off the Champs Elysée.

She calls one day to ask if I'd like to have cocktails with Max Blouet, who runs the George V. I'm a bit wary. Is this a pitch for a puff piece about the George V? But I'm curious about Max Blouet, who has a reputation as an hotelier par excellence, and so on this afternoon we are sitting in the George V bar. Phebe, Max Blouet, and I.

Soon we are talking about the hotel business in general. Max Blouet has three or four sons, and they are at the moment working in hotels around the world. A first-rate hotel manager in the luxury trade, he tells me, must speak at least three languages fluently, so he has one son in Latin America, one in London, one in Lausanne. He recommends French, English, and Spanish, rather than German, as the third most important language. No one realizes how much of the earth is populated by Spanish-speaking people, he tells us, and how often rich Venezuelans, Argentinians, and Chileans travel.

Before a man is ready to manage a hotel, Mr. Blouet goes on, he must work in every area of hotel life: in the kitchen and dining rooms, in the bars and room service, as a valet or maid, at the front desk, in reservations, at the concierge desk, in book-keeping, and, very important, in the housekeeping department. Housekeeping is more than just changing sheets, he empha-sizes. Guests must feel comfortable in their rooms and have whatever they need from a brighter lightbulb to an extra towel readily and speedily available.

Would I like to see his kitchen? M. Blouet asks, and we are off to a huge immaculate bright kitchen area. Here are men chopping vegetables for salads, making hors d'oeuvres; over there a chef is concocting a white sauce, a cook basting fowl, and on the other end of the room, the pastry cooks.

We stand behind a line of young men in white uniforms and white chef's hats working at a long table. They are making croissants for tomorrow's breakfast. One of them catches my eye. He is taller than the others, his cap is set at a rakish angle, and his sleeves are rolled up to display two huge tattoos, one of a ship and one of the Stars and Stripes.

Max Blouet smiles. No, this isn't one of his usual pastry chefs, he tells me, he is an American soldier, a corporal in the air force, on temporary assignment to the George V.

I've got my story. I ask M. Blouet if I can speak to the young man, and he calls him over. He's a big fellow, 210 pounds maybe, with bulging forearms and a lopsided shy grin. He introduces himself, Corporal Gadowski or something of the sort. He's a Polish boy from Bridgeport, Connecticut. I'm from

Connecticut I tell him, and he shakes my hand vigorously, so happy to see someone from home, but confesses he's never heard of Sharon, the small town in the northwest corner of the state that I come from.

As a teenager, Gadowski was an amateur boxer. His father ran a small grocery store in Bridgeport. When he was eighteen he enlisted in the air force and thinks he will make a career of it. Between his boxing, which made him popular with his sergeants since he brought glory to the unit in interunit matches, and his cooking, which made him popular with the officers, he had had a good service life.

Gadowski had learned to cook from his mother, and somewhere along the line his cooking had greatly pleased a gourmet air force colonel. The colonel had seen to it that when he got a new assignment, Gadowski did, too. The colonel was now a general, assigned to NATO headquarters, and he had asked Max Blouet, whom he knew well, if he would let Gadowski work in his kitchen for six weeks and teach him some culinary refinements. Max Blouet had agreed, and Gadowski had been delighted. It was a change from barracks life, and Paris, let's face it (this with a leer), was Paris, and he was learning some very useful things.

His plan was to stay in the air force for twenty years, then retire on a pension and open his own French restaurant in Bridgeport, a good life for a boy whose only assets growing up had seemed to be his fists.

It made a great story. Particularly the picture that Delvac took of Gadowski kneading pastry with his tall chef's hat a-kilter, his broad, lopsided grin, and his right hand upraised in a V-for-victory salute.

Cuisine, à la Russe

Max Blouet's kitchen had absolutely nothing in common with the only other hotel kitchen I became familiar with in France, which had been on that earlier visit to Paris in 1948, with my sister Patricia. Our view of France and the French countryside on that trip was through a distinctive Russian prism thanks to Father and Mother's good friend, and our daily companion and guide, Valerian Bibikoff.

To Bibikoff the first and paramount wonder of the world, in a league all its own, was the cathedral of Chartres. So any jaunt out of Paris, no matter in what direction, tended to begin or end with a visit to Chartres. At that gripping moment on the drive from Paris to Chartres when the cathedral is suddenly there, in front of you, etched tall against the sky, Bibi would invariably slam on the brakes (to the consternation and furious horn-blowing of any car to our rear), pull off the road, and turn to us: "Say it is beautiful!" he would roar. "It is beautiful!" we would chorus, and only then could we proceed on our journey.

Coming home from Chartres, we passed not too far from Versailles and Bibi took to stopping at a small hotel, the Hôtel du Bon Séjour, where he assured us they served a splendid tea. On the first occasion, Patricia and I were served on the terrace with the handful of other hotel guests and visitors. But on subsequent visits, and there were many, Bibikoff marched us right past the reception desk and into the hotel kitchen, a large, dim room, light years in spirit from the George V's neon-lighted, spit-polish-clean culinary emporium. The Bon Séjour's kitchen held a large double sink, a massive pre–World War II ice box-turned-refrigerator, and an old-fashioned wood stove.

Strings of onions hung from the ceiling. A large, rough wooden table occupied the center of the room and at its far end sat an old man in chef's hat and long white apron, peeling potatoes which he dropped into a large pan of water.

Bibi astonished us by snapping to attention, and saluting smartly, all but clicking his heels. He introduced us to the cook, who had, in an earlier life, been the Russian general in command of the division to which Valerian Bibikoff's regiment was attached in the final days of the war that would bring down both the Russian and the German imperial dynasties.

"Sit down, Valerian," said the general, "and have some tea." (This was one of the very few White Russian haunts we visited with Bibi where vodka was not served.) The general, I can't remember his name but it might have been Chadinoff, was a gentle soul, distinguished-looking despite his chef's hat, tall, lean, with bushy brows and brown eyes, his hair still more pepper than salt. He stood, wiped his hands on his apron, and shook hands with us both, then asked a scullery maid to bring us tea. She brought a cloth to cover the other end of the table and Bibi, Trish, and I drank our tea and ate the delicious pâtisseries we were offered while the general went on with his work.

He was content, he told us, and had fallen in good hands. The Bon Séjour was run by a White Russian couple. He had a nice room on the third floor, with plenty of space for his pictures and books. And no worries. The hotel was small so he was not overworked and had plenty of time to read and listen to music. "I am also," he smiled, "an excellent cook."

We looked forward to our visits with General Chadinoff. The conversation ranged from the old days in Russia to current politics, from gossip about the Russian community in exile to places off the beaten track that Bibi *must* take us to see while we were in France. There was general agreement on the wonders of Chartres and the vulgarity of Versailles.

One afternoon, in a nostalgic mood, General Chadinoff told us a wonderfully romantic story about Valerian Bibikoff's father, General Bibikoff, who had been Chadinoff's colonel when Chadinoff was a young officer. "Valerian's father," he told us, "was not always the martinet we took him for." As a young sub-altern, he went on, Bibikoff *père* had fallen madly in love with the daughter of a neighboring landowner at a New Year's Eve ball in the country. The young couple wanted to get married. But it was a Montague-Capulet situation: their families had been feuding for generations, a marriage was out of the question.

So one cold winter's night the young couple eloped. In the morning when their flight was discovered, the two fathers ordered out a troika and set out in pursuit, by sled, over snow-covered roads. They ran the young people down three days later, brought them home in disgrace, and had the marriage, which had been performed by a village priest, annulled, since the girl was sixteen, too young to be married without her parents' consent.

It was en route home after one of these pleasant teas that I asked Bibi when and how he had left Russia. It was in 1917, he said, when conditions at the front were frightful. Bibi was a major at the time. Rations were short, as was ammunition, and the soldiers were in rags. Everyone knew the war was lost and the country was in a state of near chaos.

"One day, I say to my soldiers, 'Go right,' and they go left. And I say, 'Go left,' and they go right," Bibi explained. "That night, I said to myself, 'Valerian, it is time to leave.'"

So he had left, deserted in fact, and made his way back to

St. Petersburg. There he learned that his sister-in-law and her children, his nephews and niece, had been killed by a mob of disaffected soldiers and peasants on a rampage of burning, looting, and murder. Valerian Bibikoff picked up his wife. I don't remember whether their son George, our friend, had been born as yet, but I think not. The younger Bibikoffs persuaded the old general and his wife that they must leave as well, and the little party made its perilous way to Odessa. There they were lucky enough to secure passage on a steamship. Bibi and his father boarded the vessel, stowed their luggage, all the valuables they had been able to carry, mostly pictures and the women's jewelry, safely in their cabins, and returned on deck. There, they noticed an old woman dressed all in black sitting by a pile of luggage on the dock. She was trying, unsuccessfully, to get someone, anyone, to help her with it. But the situation was chaotic. None of the frantic people on the dock had time for her.

The Bibikoffs went down the gangplank, careful to have their tickets in hand because two large seamen were stationed at the foot of the gangplank, warding off everyone who hadn't booked passage. They carried the old lady's luggage up and helped her find her cabin and move in.

As the ship pulled away from the dock, General Bibikoff stood by the railing watching Mother Russia recede into the distance. More realistic than his son, he knew he would never see it again. Beside him, at a small distance, stood the old lady in black they had befriended. Tears were running down her cheeks. General Bibikoff offered her his handkerchief and they started to talk. They found they knew quite a few people in common and slowly it dawned on General Bibikoff that this weary, desperate old woman was the girl he had eloped with a half-century or more before, and had not seen since.

General Bibikoff spent the last years of his life in a small apartment in London in the company of his wife and of the long-lost love he had found again on a dock in Odessa.

And a Blustery Autumn Day

It's one of those special Paris days. The sun keeps brushing its way through the clouds which skitter across the skyline, touching the dome of Les Invalides with gold, resting on the Panthéon behind it, catching the tops of small choppy waves on the Seine. Brisk autumn breezes move the fallen chestnut leaves along in fits and starts. All over the city beds of yellow chrysanthemums are fighting gallantly to hold their own against the chilly nights and doing well, thank you kindly. The huge tricolor floats under the Arch of Triumph, flapping in the breeze, but slowly in rolling waves because of its great size. Cars have been cleared from the sidewalks on the Champs Elysée in preparation for the Armistice Day parade, and the side streets are bustling with young men in uniform forming up into marching companies. We hear snatches of military marching music.

Everyone is in a good humor, moreover; whatever spot news is being made on this bright November day is not being made in Paris or in the French empire, which is our beat. It's quiet and pleasant in our grungy but on this day sun-filled office with the French windows open to let the breezes rustle through. No bells ringing, no hortatory commands have come in from London or New York for stories we don't want to write.

Nick King, Bill Landrey, and I wander out and decide to pick up a sandwich and a drink of some sort and lunch at the Buttes-Chaumont park, which is in the heart of a rundown shabby working district beyond the Gare du Nord. It's wild, built around a steep cliff of almost black rock. Tiny paths wind down the cliffs among banks of rhododendron and azalea bushes. Little waterfalls gush by, ending in a lovely lake on which swans and ducks swim. It was on this cliff that many of the highwaymen and bandits in the Middle Ages were executed and it was in these caves that the Communards made their last stand against the government in 1871. It was the indefatigable Baron Haussmann who cleared the shacks and squatter huts off the area and turned it into an enchanting park that remains, because of its location, off the tourist beat.

We pick a park bench by the lake, take out our sandwiches, and chat in desultory fashion. We are comfortable and a bit sad. Nick has just become engaged to Joan Auerbach, and although it will be a couple of months before their wedding—they will be married in France, since Joan's mother lives here—Nick is on his way out. After the wedding he and Joan will sail to New York, where he has landed a job on the editorial page of the *New York Herald Tribune*. Quite an accomplishment, but in a quiet way Nick's talents have been noted in important journalistic centers.

Bill (Wilbur G.) Landrey, a tall, soft-spoken man and a first-rate journalist, has recently succeeded Ed Korry as bureau chief, coming in from London. And already we are all buddies. Landrey will go on to become UP's chief Middle Eastern correspondent and its foreign editor, and will spend the last quarter-century of his career on the dream beat for any international journalist, as *the* foreign correspondent for a prestigious newspaper, the *St. Petersburg Times*.

But at the moment, Bill Landrey is at the receiving end of an office joke. Until he arrived the only two members of the staff who owned cars were me, with my creaky Hillman Minx, and one of UP's two photographers. One of our photographers owned a dinner jacket, which made him our society photographer; the other owned a car, which meant he met all celebrities at Orly airport, often very early in the morning. Delvac's car was even worse than mine, a lowly Deux Chevaux, with a maximum speed of about sixty kilometers an hour. But it did *"march"* more dependably than my Hillman.

Bill is determined to upgrade our vehicular profile. He has bought a brand-new undented and unscratched black Versailles—the classy car of the year—with gleaming white tires. But it has been some time since Bill has driven, and a pool is being taken in the office on whether he will pass his French driving test the first time around. The French staff is convinced that even if Bill were Sterling Moss he would flunk the test simply as a matter of French national pride.

Last night I had my friend VLT punch in a phony story on the overnight shift which Dan Halperin had duly placed on the spike for Bill to see when he came in this morning. It ran as follows:

pr—urgent

Paris, Nov. 10—(UP)—United Press Correspondent Wilbur G. Landrey, Manager for France, was arrested today

...decimating an honor company of the Republican Guard and six South American ambassadors.

after provoking a series of accidents in the fashionable Etoile section of Paris, police reported.

(plb) (more)

pr—rush

add Landrey paris xxx reported

Police reported that shortly after 10:37 (local) today a black Versailles, its whitewall tires whirling at supersonic speed, roared out of the Avenue Wagram into the Etoile apparently completely out of control.

It rammed a 52 bus, which in turn caromed off a Vespa, a baby carriage, a pushcart, and a Cadillac. The Versailles, with a man subsequently identified as Landrey at the wheel, shot through the center of the Arch of Triumph, decimating an honor company of the Republican Guard and bowling over six South American ambassadors.

The Versailles ended up plastered against the monument in the center of the Place de la Défense and Landrey was arrested.

He denied being drunk.

Police said his story was that he was "rusty" at driving.

(plb) (end)

No one enjoyed the joke more than Bill Landrey. And so it was—talking about this and that, about how the Kings would like New York after two or three years in London and Paris, and maybe even about the state of the world—that we made our way back to Rue des Italiens in time to relieve Ed Cornish, who had been holding down the desk in our absence.

Pandemonium. The spike was crawling with urgent messages that had very little to do with breaking news stories. United Press, I should probably explain here, is divided into two mutually hostile camps. There is the business end that will promise anything and everything in order to sign up a client, and the news end, which is expected to hop to and provide anything and everything an important client wants. These conflicting interests lead to battles royal which the news side invariably loses. Reynold Packard's famous *The Kansas City Milkman*, which is on the United Press index, is about this struggle.

By midnight, we were ordered to produce: (1) (for Stockholm) a thousand-word special on the Begum Aga Khan, the wife of the Aga Khan, (2) a thousand-word profile on the Abbé Pierre, the priest of the dispossessed, (3) an atmospheric piece (750 words) on daily life in Saigon, and (4) an updated obituary on Albert Schweitzer who was believed to be very ill and was our responsibility because Lambaréné, where he had built his hospital, was in the French Gabon.

Hop to it. Bill took over the news desk doing all the stories the three of us would have written normally and Nick and I divided up the specials. I drew the Begum Aga Khan (as a woman) and Abbé Pierre (as a Catholic). Nick King dredged up our 1936 guidebook of Indochina, imagined himself sitting at a café in Saigon, and produced an atmospheric masterpiece that might have fooled anyone who didn't know Saigon extremely well. Albert Schweitzer was no problem at all for Nick because

Nick knows everything. And I was able to throw in some color on that story gratis. Several weeks earlier when it was rumored that Schweitzer was terminally ill, I had been told to find out the best way to get to Lambaréné. There is no best way.

Lambaréné had no telephone at that time; it probably still doesn't. It is located seven hundred miles by river from Libreville, the capital, and there are no scheduled river trips between the two places. The only fast way to get to Lambaréné is by bush plane, if you can find one. *Bonne chance.* We all say a silent prayer that Schweitzer will outlive our stay on the Paris desk lest we find ourselves making like Stanleys.

We had it all wrapped up by 7:30 P.M., amazing what you can do when you don't want to work overtime, and celebrated with a particularly delightful dinner à trois at Le Petit Riche.

And so to bed. It had been a lovely day.

Chantilly and a Golf Championship

I am reading Robert Ahier's report of the first round of the French Amateur International Golf Championship and I am aghast. "What, Bob," I say, "is this all about?" and I quote from his copy: "Sebastián hit the ball smartly with his iron racquet so that it rose rapidly into the air transvaulting the sandy bunker to pose itself nicely on the green." Bob giggles. "I thought that was rather poetic." "It may be poetic," I say sternly, "but it isn't golf."

Bob has reported that Sebastián, the pride of Spain, lost his first match to the French defending champion, but when I ask him what was the score he doesn't know. I try another tack.

When did they leave the course? He thinks hard, but nothing comes to him. I give him a hint. It must have been after the ninth hole. He reconsiders. Now he remembers. His face brightens. They walked off after the thirteenth hole, which is the hole closest to the clubhouse, which made it easy for Robert to phone in the result for the anxious Spanish audience. I explain to Bob that if the match ended on the thirteenth hole it was probably a 6 and 5 win, meaning that the Frenchman was then six holes ahead and there were only five holes left to play. Bob breaks into a broad smile. "Peets," he says, "you are so comPétent [that's how he pronounced it] in explaining things." Bob, it turns out, thinks that three putts are better than two, and can't understand why golfers need so many racquets when tennis players can do with just one. Tennis he understands.

But Ahier is our sports correspondent, and since this year three members of the Walker Cup team are playing in the French International as well as a young air force lieutenant, Joe Conrad, who electrified the golfing world two weeks earlier by winning the British Amateur, New York decreed that we give Chantilly our full attention. Which is how come Ahier was assigned the story. We went together to Bill Landrey and suggested that I replace Ahier in the field since I was familiar with tournament golf and had even once played in the U.S. Women's National Amateur (with about the same success as Sebastián).

Unfortunately it rained hard the last three days of the tournament. My imperméable which is what the French call a raincoat, was only too perméable. My professional colleagues, Hudson of AP, Glasset of AFP, Crawley of Reuters, and lovely Victor of Extel, laughed heartily that first day when they were at lunch at a small café and I was standing in the rain outside the post office

Putting one-handedly, using
the other to hold an umbrella
over his head.

with a mound of twenty-franc coins trying to dictate the morning events to a reluctant Robert Ahier, who asked me to explain and spell every word I used that wasn't "and" or "but." It was the only phone available to me since my colleagues had staked claims to all the other nearby pay phones in town the day before. And of course the French post office is closed from 12 noon to 2 P.M., hence the outdoor phone. But when the ordeal was over they invited me to join them in a quick *fine à l'eau* since I wouldn't have time for lunch.

The star of the tournament turned out not to be the Walker Cup golfers, or even likable, red-haired young Joe Conrad, but an irrepressible college sophomore from Florida called Don Bishplinghoff. Don wouldn't know what the phrase meant, he spoke no French, but he brought to the tournament a certain *"je m'en foutisme"*—"I couldn't care less"-ism—that was enchanting to us of the press and deeply puzzling to the French. He would putt one-handed, using the other hand to hold an umbrella over his head. He had a long, loping stride and occasionally took a loose practice shot as he walked toward his ball and then hit it without stopping long enough even to take his stance. His approaches "transvaulted" every trap they were meant to and his putts regularly hit the back of the cup and fell in. On Saturday, two rounds were scheduled, the quarter- and semifinals after the Friday afternoon rounds were scrubbed because of the rain.

Friday evening, Don and Joe Conrad, the only two Americans still in the tournament, went out for dinner and played gin rummy late into the night. Bishplinghoff found when he returned to his small hotel that it was locked up tight so he went back to Joe Conrad's, curled up on the floor, and slept most peacefully.

Next day, fresh as a mountain stream, he won both his matches only to be defeated in the finals by the steady, serious French defending champion who had also been Sebastián's nemesis. Both UP and AP had worked themselves into a frenzy by the quarterfinal round and ordered us to file the nine-hole scores at the turn. But the ninth green was about half a mile from the clubhouse so Harvey Hudson (the AP man) and I agreed to phone in the ninth-hole results at the end of the thirteenth hole where the green was right by the clubhouse. We figured New York would never know the difference if our calls came in at the same time and it would save us a whole lot of legwork.

The last two or three days of the tournament I drove Glasset back into town. He lived not far from Rue Eugène Delacroix. It was a contact that proved most useful a month or so later. A story from Moscow about a weight-lifting contest arrived over the wire in French for some reason. Some classes were described, in the French version, as "press and lift" or "jerk and clean," for which no English translation came easily to mind. I couldn't find Ahier anywhere and finally in desperation remembered Glasset. I called him. He was vastly amused and led me kindly through the intricacies of Olympic-class weight lifting, making them understandable to an English-speaking audience.

That particular stint on the night desk was a sporting night-mare. I remember writing a spirited account of the finals of a classical international billiards tournament which either everyone understood or no one understood, because we received no brickbats from London or New York.

St. Firmin Revisited

Covering the Chantilly tournament had been great fun, not only because it meant getting away from the office for three days but because of the happy memories it evoked. Although I didn't remember the configuration of a single hole, I had played the course as a child along with my brothers John and Jimmy and my older sister, Aloïse.

In the spring of 1933 Father had moved the entire family from Paris to a little town called St. Firmin, right next door to Chantilly. For us country children it had been a heavenly spring and summer before cold reality hit that fall when the whole family moved to England and Aloïse and I were sent to St. Mary's convent in Ascot and John and Jimmy to the Oratory Preparatory School in Windsor.

So, on an impulse, after calling in the final story on the last evening of the tournament, I drove to St. Firmin and rang the bell at the gate of the Château de St. Firmin. In due course it was opened by a gardener—but not the surly Félix that I had known. I told him that my family had spent a summer at the château when I was a child and asked, hesitantly, if it would be all right for me to take a quick look around. He could not have been more pleasant. He opened wide the gate and told me that the house was closed at the moment—the family was away on vacation—but that certainly I was welcome to walk around the grounds if I liked. He led me to the front of the house, tipped his beret, told me to call when I wanted to get out, and returned to his mowing.

The château—it was really more of a manor house than a château—looked cold and uninviting, with shutters tightly covering the tall French doors that I remembered always open to the terrace, Nana sitting in the shade rocking a pram in which baby Maureen lay, while her older brothers and sisters, giggling and laughing, ran in and out.

The château sat on a hillside overlooking a lake, which seemed diminished to my grown-up eyes, and the pitch of the lawn steeper, but two swans patrolled its waters haughtily as had their predecessors twenty years earlier. The lake was small, but seemed large to us as children. It was fed by a stream that eventually joined the canal leading into the moat in which the monstrous carp feed around the Château de Chantilly. The lake was plenty large enough for adventurous excursions in the canoe, which only the big ones, John and Aloïse, were allowed to use, and a big flat-bottomed boat which was propelled by long poles, at the end of which were Jimmy, Jane, and me, the next three in line.

It was into this lake that Aloïse and John had dumped poor M. l'abbé Motte, the young curate who came out from Paris once a week that summer to give us catechism lessons since John and I were preparing for our Solemn Holy Communions. He had waded ashore—he didn't know how to swim—with his heavy wool soutane floating around him on the top of the water to the delight and hilarity of us younger fry, and had been forced to spend the night because his cassock did not dry in time for him to catch the last train to Paris.

The mellowness of that evening encouraged M. l'abbé Motte to ask Mother if it would be all right if he brought his Parisian catechism class to the château for a day in the country because *les pauvres petits*, they didn't know what country life was all about. Certainly, said Mother. He must bring them out and she would prepare a *pique-nique* for them and they could take rides in the boats and go swimming. But, of course, they didn't know how to swim, and M. l'abbé Motte wrung promises from John and Aloïse that they wouldn't upset the canoe because, whereas he was tall enough to wade ashore, his charges were not.

They arrived, all boys, in a big wheezing bus. They wore the short shorts of the French schoolboys of that era, and the littler ones had on their black pinafores. We had borrowed Félix's flatboat to augment our fleet for the occasion. After the initial shyness had worn off we had some glorious splashing fights with one boat taking off from one bank, one from the other, meeting in the middle, like medieval jousters, and everyone leaning over the side and splashing water onto the other boat while the grown-ups on the bank called, "*Mais faites attention. Mais soyez gentille. Mais pas trop fort,*" to which we paid no attention at all. The boys loved the American-style picnic with its fried chicken, potato chips, and cream cheese and jelly sandwiches (Mother had decided peanut butter might be too much of a culture shock), and, of course, ice cream cones and cake.

Then the asthmatic bus crept back through the gate and a silence fell over the crowd. The boys got into line to get back into their bus and M. l'abbé Motte led them in a cheer. "Eep, Eep" (M. l'abbé Motte) and "oorrah Madame Buquelet" (the boys), three times repeated. Then each, in turn, shook hands

with Mother and bobbed his thanks, and the bus pulled slowly
out into the road.

I remembered that incident and so many others of that mellow and happy summer in the gathering dusk as I drove back
into Paris. I resolved to return, with a camera, on one of my
jaunts with Mina and take a picture to send to Mother and
Father, but I never did.

Dien Bien Phu

When the cease-fire was declared in Korea in 1953, editors in
search of war stories turned their attention to French Indochina
where Ho Chi Minh had been battling for independence for
seven years. Suddenly the struggle in Indochina became front-
page news, the one spot on the globe where Communists and
non-Communists were locked in armed conflict. And we in the
Paris bureau donned our battle helmets and became instant war
correspondents at a ten-thousand-mile remove from the action.

The story—the insurrection which had been upgraded to
war level given the absence of any other major war—reached
its dramatic heights with the siege and capture by the Vieminh
(an earlier version of the Vietcong) of a remote fortress called
Dien Bien Phu. The French had seized and fortified a position
in a small valley on the Laotian border about three hundred
kilometers from Hanoi. They fortified a central command
post, placed outflanking strong points around it along the base
of the valley, and built a small airstrip that would be used to
resupply the fort and bring out the wounded should the Vietminh's General Giap be so foolish as to attack. Colonel Chris-

tian de la Croix Castries, who would be promoted to general in the course of the siege, was in command.

Most news from Indochina came in to the UP bureau in Paris via the Agence France-Presse wire. AFP was an agency of the French government and the conduit of most reports from French military headquarters in Hanoi. We embellished these stories with gleanings from the local papers and an occasional assist from our two stringers in Saigon; but the news they sent in was usually irrelevant and almost invariably late.

Hammered by New York, we were ordered to run not two or three stories a day but as many as five or six as the battle heated up. To the amazement of the French, who had simply assumed that the Vietminh would be unable to bring up the kind of artillery needed to blast through the French fortifications, Giap managed to do so. Hundreds of Vietminh troops wheeling heavily loaded bicycles pushed tons of Chinese military equipment through narrow trails and up steep hills. They dug deep caves in the hillsides surrounding Dien Bien Phu until their concealed and well-protected guns dominated the valley floor.

On March 13, 1954, they launched their first suicide attacks on several outlying strongpoints. Black-clad enemy soldiers threw themselves across barbed wire so that their fellows could use their bodies as bridges. Others drove mines under the outposts while the hidden guns in the hills plastered the area. French fighter planes tried in vain to knock out the Vietminh artillery, but with little success; French pilots flew suicide missions onto the airstrip with supplies; air force medical teams came in by helicopter to treat and bring out the more seriously wounded. Two outposts, Béatrice, and then Gabrielle, fell in the first couple of days.

On March 17, reading through a long, long story on the AFP wire about that day's attacks I learned that the last medical evacuation plane to get into the fort had been destroyed by enemy artillery. The strip was no longer safe for use and in future Dien Bien Phu would have to be supplied by parachute drop.

Way down in the story, about the twenty-fifth or twenty-eighth take, AFP gave the names of the medical evacuation team now stranded in the doomed fort: two doctors and a nurse, Lt. Geneviève de Gallard-Terraube.

I gave a whoop. "There's a woman in Dien Bien Phu," I hollered to Nick, and put out a bulletin: "French Air Force nurse trapped in Dien Bien Phu." We hit the story hard. By morning we had the wounded calling her an "angel of mercy." Soon the world was hearing about an angel "who does not wear wings or a halo, but borrowed army fatigues and a steel helmet." And so was born the Angel of Dien Bien Phu, who became instant headline news the world over.

We called Geneviève's mother and broke the news to her. She replied to our call with great dignity and asked us to join her in praying for her daughter's safety. She thanked us for our call and we promised to let her know if we received any further word on Geneviève's situation. The Gallard-Terraubes, Nick King discovered and later wrote in an amusing article on agency coverage of the Indochina war, "had lived in genteel obscurity since the day her [Geneviève's] ancestor had posed for the Jack of Diamonds during the reign of Louis XI."

In the couple of days before the fall of Dien Bien Phu, Hanoi imposed a total blackout on news from the front. Only communiqués issued by military headquarters in Hanoi would be passed by the cable office. Correspondents were barred from filing any other stories of any kind from Hanoi while the blackout lasted.

On the afternoon of May 7, Jack Schmeil and I were alone in the office. The Agence France-Presse ticker was spewing masses of copy that said very little. Suddenly there was a "FLASH," AFP's equivalent of one of our bulletins. "Military headquarters in Hanoi," it said, "has announced that the garrison of Dien Bien Phu has accomplished the mission that has been given it." This was followed by another ringing of the bells, and we were told that the previous flash was *"annulée,"* canceled. Then the bells rang again. "FLASH. Military headquarters in Hanoi has announced that the garrison of Dien Bien Phu has accomplished the mission that *had* been given it."

I called Jack over, and we studied the flash. The only difference was the tense: "that *has* been given it" was now "that *had* been given it." The mission, whatever it was, was now a thing of the past. Even at times of major tension the French insist on getting their grammar right

"I think Dien Bien Phu has fallen," I said. Jack agreed. That could be the only reason for that change in tenses—present to past—we both reasoned. But did we dare announce it to the world on such slim grounds?

We did, but with decided trepidation. "Bulletin: Dien Bien Phu Falls," and then we hung in tight while all over the world editors tore out front pages. It was five, maybe ten minutes, with London and New York screaming for official confirmation, before that blessed Agence France-Presse announced that Premier Joseph Laniel had called an emergency meeting of the French Chamber of Deputies at 1900 hours that evening; it was a Friday, by which time ordinarily the deputies would have dispersed for the weekend. "M. Laniel would have an important announcement to make."

General de Castries and ten thousand of his men, including Geneviève de Gallard-Terraube, had surrendered to General Giap earlier that afternoon. Another seven thousand of the original garrison were dead, wounded, or missing. These final defenders of Dien Bien Phu and a handful of other French POWs who had survived Vietminh captivity would be released following the Geneva Conference. The Angel of Dien Bien Phu, whose gesture in writing to thank Ho Chi Minh for the care given the wounded prisoners was not appreciated in a France still bitter over the defeat, was given a ticker tape parade on Broadway some months later.

Jack and I were the heroes of the day. UP had beaten Rox (AP) on the surrender story by better than fifteen minutes. AP did its best to find out how we had gotten the beat, but never did. Had Jack and I been wrong we would have been fired out of hand. As it was we both received letters of commendation from UP President Hugh Baillie (in lieu of a raise).

Lilli Marlene

Several months later, after the Geneva Conference in which Vietnam was divided into two separate and independent nations, North and South, and after the ninety-day grace period in which those in North Vietnam who opposed Communism were permitted freely to move south—nearly half a million, most of them Roman Catholics, adopted this option—came the formal turnover of the country to Ho Chi Minh. The very last

French troops on Indochinese territory after France's long dom-
ination of the area were a French Foreign Legion regiment.
They assembled for the final retreat at Haiphong, the port city
of Hanoi, which would now become Ho's capital. The French
marched slowly through the streets of Haiphong, and as they did
so, the tricolor disappeared from balconies and flagposts, to be
replaced by the black Vietminh flag. One hundred yards behind
the Legionnaires came the small black-uniformed Vietminh
troops who had brought proud France to her knees. They ranged
themselves along the pier as the Legionnaires climbed the gang-
planks to the troopships that would take them back to France or
to one of her outposts in Africa or the Pacific. As they boarded
the ships the soldiers sang "Lilli Marlene"—in German.

A barely noted irony of history: France's last defenders in
Indochina were Germans who had enlisted in the Legion,
many of them to avoid war crimes charges after World War II.

Not that France had gone unscathed. Indochina had cost
her the flower of her army, killing the equivalent of one entire
graduating class of St. Cyr, France's West Point, every year the
war went on.

The Whirlwind that Was Mendès-France

The fourth republic had never seen anything quite like Pierre
Mendès-France, dubbed "PMF" by his supporters in emulation
of Franklin Delano Roosevelt's "FDR." They boasted that
PMF would do for France what Roosevelt had done for Amer-
ica in the Great Depression. He would put an end to the
Indochina war, which was draining France of resources and of

its finest young men, and get on with the job of restoring the nation to its rightful position in the world.

France at large looked at the swarthy Jewish parliamentarian who was named prime minister in the bitter days following the fall of Dien Bien Phu with mingled hope and distrust. Nine years of vacillation under the Fourth Republic had taught the nation to distrust all politicians, but PMF was set in a different mold. PMF had had an untarnished war record in the resistance to the Nazi occupation of France. He had been a supporter of Charles de Gaulle in good times and bad. Here was a new broom that might, just might, sweep the cobwebs away and let France be France again. He made them a promise: he would bring an end to the war in thirty days, or resign. The citizens were willing to give him a chance.

Mendès-France kept his first promise, summoning the world's leaders, including President Dwight Eisenhower, to an emergency conference in Geneva under the gun. Unless they made peace he was out of there. A treaty was signed. It would result in the partition of Vietnam and France's withdrawal from all of Indochina. It took care of the immediate crisis but led eventually to America's tragic military involvement in Vietnam and the internal devastation that conflict brought to the United States.

PMF was unprepossessing in appearance. He looked a bit like Polichinelle (the Punch of the French Punch and Judy shows) with his heavy dark brows, heavy beard, and great hooked nose. But he had a dramatic flair and some messianic impulses. He was not afraid to take on France's sacred cows, including its love affair with wine.

Frenchmen drank too much wine, Mendès-France declared,

it was unhealthy. What they should do, and most particularly what their children should do, was: Drink Milk.

Frenchmen could not believe their ears. Milk was for babies and most French babies were weaned of the habit the minute they got off their mother's breast. The man was an idiot. "Ce n'est pas sérieux." But Mendès-France *was* serious. And France's highly centralized bureaucracy, particularly the education bureaucracy, snapped sharply to attention. If PMF said children should drink milk they would be made to drink milk in school, their parents being perceived quite rightly as less than trustworthy in this regard. With a great harrumph it was announced that henceforth milk would be on the menu in school.

The mayor of a small town about twenty-five miles south of Paris whose name and location escape me saw an opportunity for national attention here and announced dramatically that at 1600 hours the following Monday the children attending the town school would drink milk. He invited the press to attend this beginning of a new day for the children of France. Of the press, only two took up his invitation, Delvac, the UP photographer, and I.

It was a terrible October day, cold driving rain, black skies, and gusts of wind tearing the last leaves from the trees. We were in Delvac's Deux Chevaux—he refused to have anything to do with my Hillman—and the light little car lurched from side to side of the road as the wind butted it. The top was insecure and drips of cold rain seeped in, leaving us both in damp discomfort.

By the time we arrived at the mairie, we were unhappy campers. But our welcome was warm. The mayor was delighted that the international press had made the journey all the way from Paris for this great occasion. He hustled us into his office and opened a bottle of red wine to take the chill off our bones, or perhaps we would prefer a little glass of cognac? No, the wine would do, and it did indeed warm the cockles.

Then it was across the street to the schoolhouse, where we were greeted by the principal and a couple of teachers. They ushered us into a gloomy, cold refectory with a long wooden table in the center of the room, and a dozen or more chairs set around it. Each place at the table held a round soup bowl. There were three or four bowls of sugar in the center of the table.

At a signal, a door opened and a dozen or more, perhaps fifteen or sixteen little boys and girls wearing black pinafores over their school clothes, marched in and took their places at the table, standing behind their chairs. At another signal, they pulled out the chairs noisily and sat down. Some glanced at us curiously. Some giggled nervously, but with the eyes of the mayor and the principal on them, they maintained a certain decorum. Again the door opened and two women came in carrying large pitchers of steaming hot milk, which was poured into the soup bowls. The children were invited to make the drink more palatable by putting as much sugar as they liked into the milk. Then they were told to drink.

Most picked up the bowls and, with exaggerated looks of disgust and despair, took small sips and then, finding the sugary warm milk less appalling than they had been led to believe, drank it down. A couple of boys made gagging sounds, but they were muted.

All of them drank but Monique. Monique, a small solemn eight-year-old with heavy dark across-the-brow bangs, pressed her lips tightly together and refused to drink. Monique, you must drink your milk, a teacher rebuked her. *"Non."* Monique, M le maire desires you to drink your milk. *"Non."* Monique, thundered the principal, the prime minister of France orders you to drink your milk. A shake of the head. A muttered *"Non."* The hint of a tear, but no sign of surrender in the unblinking round brown eyes that confronted us all. Monique had the determination of a Joan of Arc. Mendès-France might be the undisputed leader of the French nation, but he wasn't going to tell Monique Bonnard what to do. And he didn't. No, said Monique to PFM and in fact, no, said the nation to him not many months later.

The mayor got his story, but it wasn't the one he had planned.

Time to Go Home

Suddenly it is time to go home. One minor consideration is the six-day week, which is getting me down. To be so close to everything I want to see in Europe but with no time to see it. But mostly it is because on his last visit to Paris in September my father had seemed markedly worse. He'd had three or four strokes, two of them very bad indeed, and it has been driven home to all of us that our days with him are limited. Finally, in the incoming mail early in December I had received a slim blue-bordered magazine printed on butcher paper, Issue One, Volume I, of the magazine my brother Bill has been raising money to start for well over a year. It is called *National Review,* A Journal of Conservative Opinion. I leaf through it briefly. Except for pieces by family members, my brother Bill and sister Aloïse Heath, the only names of authors I am familiar with are James Burnham, whose *Managerial Revolution* I studied at Smith, and Willmoore Kendall, who was a professor of Bill's at Yale.

Shortly thereafter Bill is on the phone asking me to return to New York and work on *National Review*, which is big on professors but short on working journalists. I wonder whether the pace of a weekly magazine won't seem a bit slow after eight years, both here and earlier in New York, of working on the basis of a deadline every minute. I have no inkling, as I read that first issue of what a reader would later call "a blue-bordered haven in the desert of slanted news," that I will spend the next thirty-seven years—which is longer than I have lived—helping make *National Review* a major player in America's turn to the right, the Reagan election, and the end of the cold war.

We're terribly shorthanded, so when I tell Arthur Higbee, my third bureau manager in a little over two years, that I am leaving I give him a full month's notice. To my astonishment I am offered an immediate $15-a-week raise to stay, but it's too late, the decision is firm, and I am now chomping at the bit for a different kind of life.

Still, as I write Mother, I am suddenly overwhelmed by nostalgia. Just as in those first days in Paris I find myself wandering the streets, savoring their animation, smelling with pleasure the malodorous stenches of narrow twisting Left Bank alleys, enjoying vicariously the chatter of black-clothed old women sitting on benches in the Luxembourg and Tuileries gardens. I want to store all that away as if I were never to see Paris again.

Memories, Most Golden, One Sad

But I'm also overwhelmed by newer memories, a golden October afternoon in the valley of the Marne. Verdier has asked Nick King and me to a Sunday lunch with his wife. Verdier is UP's jack of all trades. He's tall and blond, probably in his early fifties. He wears a workman's blue uniform around the premises and is the man you call when anything goes wrong, from a grumpy pencil sharpener to a malfunctioning teletype machine. He's there when the lights go out, when the toilet is clogged, when a key is bent on your typewriter. "*Ce n'est pas sérieux*," he will say and proceed to put it to rights.

Lunch is one of those leisurely affairs that will take two or three pleasant hours. It is served in the grape arbor outside the kitchen and we play musical chairs around the table as the sun bores through the leafy covering and catches an eye. Verdier laughs and tells Nick about the morning he found me in near panic. It was the day that Eisenhower was arriving in Switzerland for the Geneva Conference. It had been arranged that news of his arrival would be filed from Geneva directly to Paris where we would open up the key and let it move swiftly on to London.

But on that morning, Verdier is telling us with great enjoyment, Mlle. Buckley has opened the mail and found that the Electricité et Gaz of France will turn off all power on Rue des Italiens for four hours to make needed repairs. I was in a state of shock. "But Verdier tells me," I break in with a grin, "that it is not *sérieux*," and it turns out not to be. Verdier finds an old generator from the end-of-the-war days. It needs as much oil as the Tin Woodman of Oz, but by nine o'clock (Eisenhower is scheduled to touch down shortly after ten) the generator is sitting on the balcony and generating enough power to keep a few lights on and one teletype machine working. The arrival bulletin goes through without a hitch. So who cares that the whole thing blows up shortly afterwards; we have a merry little fire out on the balcony. We all laugh and lift our wine glasses in salute to the Verdiers, long may they wave.

I remember, too, several suppers at the Ahiers' at which six- or seven-year-old Patrick was invariably impossible. Bob would indulge the boy, a kinetic child with a mop of his mother's curly blond hair, and fail to back up his wife, Blondie, when she tried to rebuke the child. A dozen years later, young Patrick, now at the Sorbonne, would leave home to live with a girl, a fellow student. Boys will be boys, Bob commented. But when, three months later, the girl left Patrick for someone else, Patrick was devastated. He had never been crossed or deprived of anything he wanted. He shot his brains out, age eighteen. That shot also brought down Bob Ahier, who was dead a few months later, very prematurely, the medical diagnosis, whatever it was, notwithstanding, of a broken heart. Like all of Bob's friends, I was shattered by his death.

Then there was the Easter Vigil Mass VLT took me to. This was long before Vatican II, but some of the French clergy were experimenting with new forms of worship, among them a Mass on Holy Saturday. We go to VLT's little church in a workman's district, enter in almost pitch dark. At midnight, the lights flash on. The priest chants: Christ Is Risen, Christ Will Come Again. The congregation lights the candles it has received on entering and forms a procession moving outside, candles flickering in the breeze, to escort the priests and altar boys who are bringing the Blessed Sacrament back to the Sanctuary, and the Vigil light, which has been extinguished since Good Friday, is ceremoniously relit.

We climb the four flights of steps to VLT's apartment after

Fritures at a tiny restaurant overlooking
the river at Moret-sur-Loing.

Mass and have a quiet collation, just the four of us, VLT, his
wife, and the neighbor who has stayed with the three children
while we were at Mass. I wonder how VLT's wife manages
those steps with three children, one still in a pram.

The flying visit to Rome, leaving at 3 P.M. Friday and returning after lunch on Sunday, arrived in time for the 6 P.M. to
midnight shift. Tish Baldrige, who is working for Ambassador
Clare Boothe Luce, has invited me because brother Jim and
his wife Ann will be there for the weekend. Jim has been
exploring for oil in Libya. We dine Friday night at a villa on a
hill just outside the city. It was once lived in by Mussolini's
mistress, Clara Petacci. Saturday we attend a reception in the
residency at which four cardinals are present. Mrs. Luce wears
a graceful long off-white lace dress and long white gloves, the
only touch of color a cardinal-crimson sash and cardinal-

crimson evening slippers. Time for an early lunch on Sunday in the Borghese gardens after Mass at Santa Maria Maggiore.

A Christmas with the Rigbys in their tight little apartment near the Rue de Rennes. As I arrive shortly after noon, Frenchmen in their black Sunday best can be seen leaving the local boulangeries, each gingerly carrying a platter on which sits a smoking goose or turkey. Bakers' ovens on this day work overtime. First they bake the morning breads, then the geese and turkeys that are too big to fit in the small ovens in the average Paris apartment of the time. The streets have never smelled so sweet.

Or the glorious four days I spent with the Rigbys at Soulac-sur-Mer on the Bordeaux estuary. After breakfast every morning we go for a swim. There are no waves since we are not on the ocean but the water is still ocean salty. At noon, the nurse takes the boys home for lunch and their nap and Bob, Amy, and I repair to a seaside stand and sit on a rickety porch by a rickety table. The patron brings us each six oysters he has just fished out of their bed of ice and expertly opened and several quarters of lemon. Our lips are still salty from the swim. We eat the oysters and wash them down with a pale, almost white, glass of Bordeaux ladled from a barrel of wine sunk into the sand in the floor of the shed, to keep it cool. Then it is home to lunch and our nap.

And the dozens of weekends with Mina Wheeler in whichever of our Hillmans is marching, during which we visit places of great and minor interest within a two-hundred-kilometer radius of Paris, which is all we can easily handle on my abridged schedule. We gaze, marveling, at the lofty vault of the cathedral at Beauvais, eat *fritures* at a tiny restaurant on the bank of a stream at Moret-sur-Loing, near Fontainebleau, run out of gas in the Forest of Campiègne (my fault, not the Hillman's), and find ourselves one afternoon perched on the ramparts of the Château Gaillard, high above the Seine, watching a performance of *Macbeth* in French by the Jean-Louis Barrault company, and nearly fall off the walls when the majestic line: "Hail, Macbeth!" rings out: *"Olà, Olà, Monsieur Macbeth."*

Good friends, good times—but also time to say good-bye. I am most particularly pleased as I write Mother in my last letter from Paris that Yves and Jean, the two copy boys, have joined with Mlle. Henri to buy me a farewell present, a saucy gold and green evening bag. I can't imagine which of the three could have thought of such a frivolity. I love it.

As I reach for the doorknob this last afternoon, Mlle. Henri rises from her seat at the switchboard. She shakes my hand, then gives me a bear hug of an embrace.

"Au revoir, Mlle. Buckley. Bon voyage et bonne chance."

I close the door leaving the clatter and the clamor behind. It's a permanent good-bye to newspaper days, but not to Paris, not ever to Paris.

—30—

AFTERWORD

by "Brother Bill," William F. Buckley Jr.

That (1956) was hardly the last time Priscilla saw Paris, which she has revisited twenty times since abandoning life there in order to help out her (baby!) brother. Yes, I was born a few years after Margaret Mary Priscilla Langford, who was the third of ten children, I coming along as sixth.

For reasons never explored even among ourselves, the children of W.F.B. and Aloïse Steiner Buckley have always been reluctant to ask favors of one another. The way it works—with us—is that Sibling A will tell Sibling B that it would be fine (useful) (wonderful) if Sibling C would undertake a particular chore or assume a particular burden. Maybe volunteer to take Sibling A to his sailboat at Lakeville Lake because she, having reached age sixteen, had a driving license. Or maybe an intermediary sibling would advise Priscilla that it would be much appreciated by younger brother A if she would extend an invitation to him and his roommate to drive up to Smith College on their holiday from school.

Of course! (A family tendency was to be compliant when

requests came in, however indirectly.) That meant for me, in a borrowed family car, an exciting fifty-mile drive to Northampton where Priscilla, a junior, was an awesome celebrity, holding down the role of managing editor of the Smith College daily newspaper. We'd get there in time to lunch with her at Hubbard House, in the company of those glamorous superachieving girls of nineteen and twenty, and then (I remember) she took us to the big toboggan run at the nearby mountain, packed with snow and ice, and we did the whirlwind ride down, emerging lusty with the sense of danger overcome and unashamed to demand of my older sister the instant sustenance of hot chocolate.

Well, yes, the day came, a dozen years later, when I suggested to sister Trish that it would be nice and useful and wonderful for the gestating weekly magazine over whose fortunes fate had placed me if Priscilla could be persuaded to leave her job with United Press in Paris and come to New York to help us put out *National Review*. So Pitts (as the reader has learned she was frequently called) came to us. In a year or two the incumbent managing editor, a distinguished lady of letters now just a little antiquated, retired, and Priscilla took over and served for thirty-seven years. *National Review*, for all that it is a highly professional journal and always read as such, was a very intimate editorial operation. I was the editor, and proprietor, Priscilla was the organizing editorial intelligence, and James Burnham was the general mentor with heavy contributions from illustrious senior writers, including Whittaker Chambers, Frank Meyer, Jeffrey Hart, and John Chamberlain. She brought with her the highly honed professional skills with which the reader of this book has been acquainted, notwithstanding her modest description of her career as a reporter for United Press. She brought also fastidious parietal habits: she was always at her desk at nine in the morning (a quaint convention exuberantly ignored by her successors). Under her direction, editorial copy moved on schedule, going to the press only after she had supervised every editorial act. We closed the magazine, in those days, on Wednesdays at six—an inflexible hour, at which the courier would leave the building clutching our precious editorial cargo, his mission being to deliver it by midnight to the printer waiting in New Haven, Connecticut.

The hectic day before—the Tuesdays—Priscilla and I and James Burnham, the workhorses of the editorial writing team, would stay on after the official closing hour, working uninterrupted on the 7,000 words of copy required to fill the editorial section. James Burnham, the austere philosopher who had agreed to leave his country life and come to *National Review* two days every week, was wholly at ease with Priscilla (they shared an office), was happy in her company, attentive to her editorial reactions, always diffidently proffered, warmed by her good humor.

At approximately nine, accompanied by whoever was also on writing duty, we would leave the building and go for dinner at any of a dozen midtown New York eateries, order food and wine and otherwise express our enthusiasm for life in general, for our work that long day in particular; record our dismay over the national and international political scene, and touch on the running amusement of that week's political events.

No one profited more from Pitts's company than the editor in chief, and our joint professional enterprise was punctuated with sallies of every kind and character. My means of proposing to Priscilla something off schedule and offbeat assumed, after a few years, a verbal ritual. I would pick up the telephone and dial her extension.

"Pitts, what 'were' you doing next Wednesday?"

"Well, I 'was' going to be here in New York, at work. What 'am' I doing?"

"You are going to Mexico for the weekend."

And off we would go, to Mexico for the weekend. Or on a sailboat to Nantucket. Or a dove-shoot in South Carolina. Or to *Gotterdämmarung* at the Met. There was that wonderful, mysterious flexibility in her iron work schedule. She was always at *National Review*, doing her work, yet somehow always available for any flight of fancy suggested by her brother.

Her good humor suffused the office. The legions of young men and women who trained under Priscilla at *National Review* do not forget the experience of working with her, even after decades. David Brooks, the author and journalist, wrote just lately in an introduction to one of my own books, "By the time I got to *National Review* in 1984, it was a convivial ship. We were all so wrapped up in admiration for managing editor Priscilla Buckley that we weren't in a mood to feud. But in the early days, apparently *NR* was like a crowded valley in the Appalachians, with rifle fire from shed to shed." Nobody ever aimed fire at Pitts.

The memory of George Will is keen, his tribute on one public occasion was ornate and expressive. "The point is that Priscilla has shown us all how to combine serious interests with an undiminished and irrepressible flair for fun. She is the flute in our conservative orchestra, who taught, by example, the compatibility of political commitment and generosity of spirit."

It was nicely summed up at *NR*'s thirtieth-anniversary dinner by our guest of honor, President Ronald Reagan. Everybody knows that presidential speeches are drafted by assistants. But this speech (as was true of most of Reagan's speeches) bore handwritten corrections, one of them accenting the passage he spoke about Priscilla Buckley. He said of her, recalling the years of political argumentation before his arrival at the White House, "Priscilla has come through all this with a reputation unchallenged for journalistic skill and professionalism, as well as the sweetest disposition on the Eastern Seaboard."

He'd have been glad to read this book, recounting her preparations for her second career.